**Keep your kids happy _and_ healthy!
Learn to make these tempting, tasty
treats . . .**

- CASHEW COOKIE CLUSTERS
- RAISIN SQUARES
- GRANOLA NUTTERS
- WALNUT SPICERS
- NO-BAKE PINK LEMONADE PIE
- CHUNKS OF CHERRIES
- COCONUT CUPCAKES
- SWEET BREAD PUDDING
- GRAPE CREAM DESSERT
- RED, WHITE, AND BLUEBERRY
    DESSERT
- ORANGE BOATS
- EASY LEMON SHERBET
- PINEAPPLE BLUES
- LIP-SMACKING BAKED PEARS
- POPCORN ON A STICK
- SNOW BARS
- SUGARLESS PEANUT BUTTER CANDY

AND DOZENS MORE!

100

Healthy

DESSERTS YOUR KIDS WILL LOVE

▲▼▲▼▲▼▲▼▲▼▲▼▲▼▲▼▲▼▲▼▲

ROBIN ZINBERG

Introduction by Beth Allen
Produced by Skylight Press

BERKLEY BOOKS, NEW YORK

100 HEALTHY DESSERTS YOUR KIDS WILL LOVE

A Berkley Book / published by arrangement with
Skylight Press

PRINTING HISTORY
Berkley edition / July 1993

ISBN: 0-425-13816-X

A BERKLEY BOOK ® TM 757,375
Berkley Books are published by The Berkley Publishing Group,
200 Madison Avenue, New York, New York 10016.
The name "BERKLEY" and the "B" logo
are trademarks belonging to Berkley Publishing Corporation.

PRINTED IN THE UNITED STATES OF AMERICA

10 9 8 7 6 5 4 3 2

Acknowledgments

I would like to thank my friends, Cynthia Cincotti, Ronnie Kars, and Rhoda Lange for pulling me out of the kitchen once in a while. My thanks to the world's best taste testers, my sons, Michael and Adam; and to my partner in everything, my husband, Barry.

Contents

An asterisk (*) indicates the recipe contains no sugar, molasses, or honey.

100

Healthy

DESSERTS
YOUR KIDS
WILL LOVE

•• 1 ••

Introduction:
Yes, Mom, Desserts
Can Be Healthy!

Contrary to popular opinion, desserts for kids can be healthy and still have kid appeal. They do not have to be laden with empty calories, sugars, and fats.

Take, for instance, that double-decker ice cream cone, dripping with cream and calories, which is a favorite snack for nearly every child. Even that treat can be made healthier yet stay just as tempting. For instance, choose a wafer cone instead of a sugar cone, then scoop in frozen low-fat yogurt or orange sherbet instead of rich chocolate ice cream. The fat and calories go down, while the kid appeal remains the same.

The facts speak for themselves: Reduce the sugars and fats in desserts and you have a dessert that's richer in nutrients, lower in things less good for you, and higher in foods that are good for you. This usually means more fruits, whole grains, and low-fat dairy products, and less butter, sugar, eggs, and cream. But it does not have to mean less kid appeal!

In childhood, we begin to form eating habits that will probably last a lifetime. Teach kids to reach for a handful of juicy strawberries instead of a candy bar, a glass of orange juice instead of a sweet soda. Gradually, the familiarity and likability of fresh fruit and fruit juices become a healthy eating habit. At the same time, those sugary candy bars will become less and less tempting as the years roll by.

Teaching your kids to like—and even to ask for—healthy desserts is what this book is all about. The recipes prove that healthy can be good, as well as good for you.

Whether your kid loves cookies, cupcakes, puddings, or shakes, we offer you a collection of healthy desserts like No-Bake Pink Lemonade Pie, Pineapple Blues, and Smiling Apples, which kids are bound to love, even though these desserts are good for them! There are Banana Ramas, Chunks of Cherries, and Fruity Cookie Fingers to fill the cookie jar and Snow Bars to put in the candy jar. Plus we have invented gelatin concoctions such as Raspberry Clouds and Strawberry Smash, fabulous frozen fantasies such as Watermelon Building Blocks and Red, White, and Blueberry Dessert, and smashing shakes with names like Shakin' Strawberries and Peachy Keen Shake. And for the kids who love to snack, we have Popcorn on a Stick and Fabulous Fruit Chillers.

There are 100 recipes in all. More than one-third of them are made with no sugar, molasses, or honey at all. These have been marked with an asterisk to make them easy to find and identify.

Read through the recipes, then pick a few to try. Just for the fun of it, let your kids and their friends help. And while they are mixing and measuring, take advantage of a teachable moment to help them recognize the healthier ingredients these recipes use. When the desserts are ready for tasting, join in. You'll find many of these wholesome treats are delicious for the whole family.

But before you head for the kitchen, take a moment to read the rest of this introduction. We help you take the mystery out of those myths pertaining to what kids will and will not eat for dessert. Next, we help you size up the facts of why it makes healthy eating sense to cut back on sugars and fats, regardless of your age. Then, finally, we take you on a trip through the market to help you find healthy dessert ingredients and to help you choose healthy ready-to-eat treats when you don't have the time to prepare desserts in your own kitchen.

Disproving Those Mysterious Dessert Myths

Since Grandmother's time and even before, dessert recipes have been handed down from family to family, generation to generation. Often, it was the seven-layer coconut cream cake that won a blue ribbon at the county fair, or a homemade strawberry shortcake with mounds of freshly whipped cream, or a rich chocolate cream pie with peaks of sweet meringue.

Whatever the desserts, the memories of our childhood remain. And many of those delicious desserts are still served today, but usually only on special occasions. Gone are the days when each meal must end with a fat-filled sweet. Here are the days when we know that alternatives exist—that each calorie, spoonful of sugar, and gram of fat we eat counts—whatever our age.

Myths can confuse us concerning whether it is really healthy to let our kids eat dessert. To help you sort out fact from fiction, here are a few of the frequently heard statements about desserts, which are actually myths, plus the real facts behind them.

MYTH # 1: Desserts must be bad for you to taste good.

For years, those towering cakes and pies or rich ice cream and cookies—all high in butter, cream, eggs, and often chocolate—were the images that first came to mind when children wanted to know, "What's for dessert?" But today, it's possible to please your child's sweet tooth with a juicy peach or a fruit-filled cookie.

MYTH # 2: All kids want for dessert is ice cream or cake.

It's a fact: We are born with a sweet tooth. In other words, we have an inherent liking for sweets. But contrary to popular opinion, that sweet tooth can be satisfied just as well by a bowl of sweet berries as a slice of fudge cake.

MYTH # 3: Kids expect something sweet after school.

Chances are, this myth grows out of those advertisements of yesteryear showing kids perched on a drugstore stool with their books nearby. In front of them was often a delicious-looking sundae or ice cream soda. And surrounding them were their smiling friends ready to take a taste or a sip.

Today, though, we know that such habits are created, not born. So it is just as easy to have your children grow up wanting—and very much liking—a yogurt or a piece of fruit for that after-school snack, instead of a sugary sweet.

MYTH # 4: A candy bar is the perfect way to cheer up kids.

Not true! In fact, if a child eats a candy bar, especially on an empty stomach, he or she will quickly experience a sugar high, followed a few minutes later by a dramatic sugar low. So, instead of cheering up your child, you may actually be causing him or her to become irritable, sluggish, and even sadder than before.

MYTH # 5: The only way I can get my children to eat their meal is to bribe them with dessert.

As previously noted, children's eating habits are created, often by following your examples. The healthy way to develop smart eating habits is to make each part of the meal interesting and tasty. Avoid tempting your children with dessert in order to get them to eat their meat and salad. It's an unhealthy habit that is hard to break. Some savvy parents prefer to serve dessert only occasionally and an hour or more after the meal.

MYTH # 6: Dessert makes a perfect reward!

Using dessert as a reward is *not* a good idea. When parents use food to comfort or to show approval for good behavior, food disorders can develop. Plus, using food as a reward can get out of hand and become an undesirable habit that children will grow to expect. Gradually, such dessert rewards create an image that a child's favorite dessert is a good thing, when the opposite may be true.

It is definitely best to separate food from emotions. Reward good behavior in other ways, like a special outing or perhaps small payment for a chore well done.

MYTH # 7: Withholding dessert is a successful way to punish kids.

Withholding dessert is simply short-term punishment that does not teach your child a behavioral lesson. Once again, it could become a habit—one that your child may regret later in life. Such habits could lead to overindulging in desserts as your child gets older.

Introducing Good-for-Them Desserts!

To be good for the crayon crowd, and even you, too, desserts must meet certain specifications. The desserts included in these pages are healthy, delicious treats. Nutritionally speaking, they are:

- Low in sugar
- Low in fat
- Nutrient-packed
- Calorie-conscious

But that's not all. To increase the kid appeal of the recipes, we have given them catchy names, such as Carrot Tops and Chocolate Chip Brittle. Many of the names remind kids of things that they are usually not supposed to eat frequently, like brownies, pies, cakes, or cookies. Such names definitely attract the younger generation.

In many cases, you will find that the desserts are baked and shaped into familiar shapes, which resemble characters and things that kids love, like Strawberry Jam Cake and Orange Boats. Not only this, they are also fun and easy to fix. So let the kids help!

Most importantly, Good-for-Them Desserts rate high on the Great Taste Scale—for kids and adults alike!

Dessert Matters

Often, parents notice that kids eat small amounts of dessert, especially in comparison to what they themselves might eat. So they tend to not worry about the types of desserts they make. Additionally, they believe that kids deserve treats too.

So why worry about what's inside those desserts? *Because it's important*—for your kids' health, and yours, too! Here are some of the reasons, backed up with the real facts:

What Your Child Eats Today Could Become a Lifelong Pattern

Even though eating fat-filled, sugary sweet foods is not addictive, in the sense that our bodies do not become physically dependent upon them, one can easily develop a liking for them over time. Eating such foods can become habit forming and can result in a not-so-healthy way of life.

Naturally, from the day we are born, we are surrounded with sweet temptations. Some of our first celebrations when we grow up are birthday parties, complete with cake and ice cream. School parties on Valentine's Day and other holidays often feature sweets. Most family gatherings such as Thanksgiving dinner normally end with a slice of pie, or maybe even two.

In fact, happy occasions often mean sweet occasions. But this doesn't necessarily have to always be the case. It's true that traditions, peer pressure, neighborhood bakeries, and trips to amusement parks seem to warrant sweet treats. But that does not mean such sweet, fat-filled treats should become a daily habit. In fact, it's up to us to make sure that our children do not develop as sweet a sweet tooth as many of us, as parents, already have.

Sugary Facts

On the average, Americans are a sugar-loving population. Approximately 25 percent of our daily calories come from sugar. This means that a six-year-old probably gets an average of about 425 calories from sugar every day. And many of those calories are served up in desserts.

For our children's sake, it pays to take a minute to review the Sugary Facts:

High-Sugar Foods Can Cause Tooth Decay

When plaque bacteria on our teeth are exposed to sugars and starches, they produce acids. If these acids are allowed to stay on our teeth—that is, if they are not washed away or brushed away quickly—they can eat away and damage the enamel on our teeth. The results? Tooth decay and cavities.

For this reason, it's never too early for children to develop a taste for tooth-friendly foods, especially at dessert time. And you can help them:

- Avoid making desserts with raisins and cookies with sweet, sticky fillings that stick to the teeth.
- When you bake a cake, cut down on the sugar. Serve a thin slice of cake with a glass of low-fat milk. The milk helps to clear the sugar from the mouth that could cause cavities.
- Pack an apple in your kids' lunch boxes, instead of fruit roll-ups, which stick to their teeth.
- Sweeten milk shakes with pureed fresh fruits like strawberries and peaches instead of sweet ice cream syrups.

High-Sugar Foods Rate Low in Nutrient Density

By definition, high calorie foods like cookies, cakes, and pies rate high in sugar calories, low in nutrients. In other words, we describe them as being low in nutrient density. On the healthier side, desserts featuring nutrient-dense foods, such as fruits, whole grains, or low-fat dairy products, are high in nutrient density. That is, they deliver good nutritional value for the calories.

Obesity Is Often Related to a Diet High in Sugar

If you let your children—or yourself—get into the habit of eating foods high in sugar, gradually they will want more and more sugary foods. That means they will be eating fewer and fewer healthy foods. Eventually, they may even find themselves adding pounds they do not want. Eating foods with too much sugar becomes an unhealthy habit that could result in obesity later in life.

Obesity can put your children in the high-risk category for several diseases like heart disease, high blood pressure, and even gallstones. Plus, there are studies that show that overweight individuals are more likely to develop diabetes.

The Highs and Lows of It All

When a person eats a candy bar or a sugar-packed dessert like a brownie, he or she gets a reaction called a sugar high, often described as a quick pick-me-up. But actually, the opposite is true.

Eating that candy bar results in a type of euphoria caused by the rapid, dramatic rise in blood glucose, the digested form of sugar. If you are a normal, nondiabetic person, your pancreas responds to this quick increase of glucose by rapidly releasing a spurt of insulin into your blood. This action causes your glucose level to fall down, resulting in a sugar low, and leaving you with low energy, which can make you irritable and even hungrier than before.

In children, this sugar high, followed a few minutes later by a sugar low, can have an even more dramatic effect than in adults. Since children react in extreme ways to biochemical changes in their bodies, they often experience noticeable mood swings as a result of such concentrated sugar intakes.

We believe it is never too early to start children on the right path to a healthy diet, so many of the recipes in this book use no sugar at all. Instead, they are often sweetened with fruits and fruit juices, which are frequently combined with complex carbohydrates, such as whole wheat flour or whole oats, which are metabolized more slowly than simple sugars.

When children eat complex carbohydrates, it takes their bodies time to digest these foods and to break them down into simpler sugars that can be absorbed into their bloodstreams. Only after this action occurs can the sugars be carried to their body cells for fuel. This slower process results in a healthier, more measured flow of sugar into the blood. This means no sugar highs and no sugar lows—just a steady level of blood glucose that gives children—and you, too—a constant amount of energy, leaving everyone feeling better in the long run.

Can Sugar Cause Disease?

By itself, sugar can not cause disease. However, eating too much sugar—combined with living certain life-styles and inheriting tendencies toward some diseases—can result in becoming unhealthy later in life.

As we have already noted, a diet high in sugar can result in obesity, and that can increase the risk of heart disease. Also, some studies indicate that too much sugar may also increase the level of triglycerides (that is, blood fats) in certain individuals. A high triglyceride level is yet another risk for heart disease.

A high-sugar diet has also been linked to gastrointestinal diseases in some people. Thus, low-sugar foods are often recommended for people suffering from such ailments as colitis, diverticular disease, and abdominal bloating after eating sugar.

For their skin's sake, children, especially those entering their teens, are smart to cut back sugars in their diet. Sugary desserts can lead to acne outbreaks and pimples in some people. On the healthier side, a balanced diet and foods low in sugars may improve skin conditions and promote an overall sense of physical well-being.

Fat Facts

It's a fact: A high level of blood cholesterol increases your chances for developing heart diseases. This is true, regardless of your age.

Today, more and more children are at risk. One out of every four children between the ages of two and eighteen has a cholesterol level that is too high. One child in twenty in America has an exceedingly high cholesterol level, one that is greater than 200 mg/dl.

So, experts now agree that children over age two should learn to eat the health-smart way: They should follow the low-fat diet recommended for everyone. Teaching children to enjoy low-fat foods can go a long way in preventing high cholesterol levels during childhood years. A habit of eating low-fat foods will also prove to be the smart way to keep children heart-healthy throughout life.

About Dietary Fats and Cholesterol

The experts agree: A diet low in dietary fats (the fats in foods) is generally considered healthier than a high-fat diet. It is scientifically established that a low-fat diet leaves you at lower risk for heart diseases.

Important, too, is cholesterol—both the cholesterol that you eat in foods like animal fats, and the cholesterol that your body produces from the other fats you eat. Generally, it is wise to eat an overall diet that is low in fats. When you do choose products with fats, most experts suggest that the fats that you do eat should be more than one-third monounsaturated fats, less than one-third saturated fats, and less than one-third polyunsaturated fats.

Why? A diet high in saturated fats will generally cause your blood cholesterol to rise; a diet low in fats, especially saturated fats, generally causes blood cholesterol to remain in control or even to decrease.

It's important to realize that fats in the foods we eat usually contain a mixture of all three types of dietary fats:

1. **Saturated fats:** animal fats such as those in butter, cheese, egg yolks, beef suet, and milk; tropical oils such as coconut oil, palm-kernel oil, and palm oil, cocoa butter (which is present in chocolate), and coconut
2. **Monounsaturated fats:** olive oil, peanut oil, peanut butter, olives, cashews, peanuts
3. **Polyunsaturated fats:** corn oil, cottonseed oil, margarine, safflower oil, soybean oil, almonds, pecans, walnuts

The Risks of That High-Fat Diet

Since children start developing lifelong eating habits at a young age, it is never too early to begin preventing diseases that may result from a high-fat diet.

Studies show that a diet high in fat can increase your risk for various diseases such as cancer, coronary heart disease, strokes, hypertension, diabetes, high cholesterol, gallstones, and arthritis. If you are overweight, the risks are even greater.

For these reasons, low-fat foods, especially low-fat desserts, make sensible heart-healthy eating!

Buying Health-Smart

Although you have to be careful, it is possible these days to buy prepared desserts without courting nutritional disaster. The key is learning to read labels.

What's on labels these days? A lot! So make an effort to use the information that is yours for the reading. On that next food shopping trip, take your kids along. Together, you can discover which foods have those extra sugars and fats hidden inside and which ones are simply packed with good-for-you things without too many fats and sugars added.

Here are some guidelines that will help you sleuth out the best dessert ingredients and ready-to-eat desserts for your whole family.

Reading the Labels for Sugar Content

It's the law: The ingredient statement must list ingredients in order of their prominence by weight, in descending order, from the most to the least. Processed foods usually carry ingredient statements, but 350 types of common foods that follow government "standards" are presently exempt from labeling requirements by the Food and Drug Administration. So products such as milk, ice cream, canned fruits, cocoa, and sweeteners do not necessarily have to carry an ingredient label, although many manufacturers do provide one.

Many foods deviate from such government standards, even though they might resemble a familiar product. Consequently, they are required to carry an ingredient statement. For instance, the new light ice creams are packed in cartons similar to those of regular ice creams, and are usually stacked next to the familiar ice cream products in the freezer case. However, they do differ. One product we found claims it contains one-third less butterfat than the regularly prepared product, which means this product deviates from the government standard for ice cream. Thus, it carries an ingredient statement, which reveals other information. We found that its number-two ingredient is sugar; its third ingredient, corn syrup. (Even though it is lower in fat, there is a lot of sugar frozen inside!)

It is always smart to read the ingredient statement carefully before you buy. The current federal food regulations direct manufacturers to list the various types of sweeteners separately. This means you must read the label slowly in order to locate all of the sweeteners inside. For instance, we picked up a box of some ready-to-eat Oatmeal Raisin Cookies. At first glance, they looked healthier than most, especially since the label boasted "Fat Free—Cholesterol Free." But do not be fooled! By reading the ingredient statement, we discovered that the first ingredient listed is sugar; the sixth, molasses; the ninth, maltodextrin; the thirteenth, dextrose. Added together, there are four sweetening ingredients inside these cookies. This means that if you buy this product, you and your kids will probably be eating a substantial amount of sugar, even though the cookies sound like they might be healthy. Instead, come home and bake up some healthy Banana Ramas (see page 52).

Finding Those Hidden Sugars

Sugar is sugar—or is it? Naturally, if the label reads "sugar," this means there is probably sucrose, or regular table sugar, inside. But that is not necessarily all! Look closely; there may be other sugars hidden there, too.

Here is a guide to help you uncover all the sugars tucked in ingredient statements:

- **Ingredients ending in *-ose* are usually sugars:** dextrose (which is another name for glucose), sucrose, high fructose corn syrups, maltose
- **Any ingredient using the word "sugar":** beet sugar, brown sugar, confectioner's sugar, invert sugar, raw sugar, turbinado sugar
- **Sweeteners with other names:** honey, molasses, maple syrup
- **Sugar alcohol products:** mannitol, sorbitol, and xylitol (absorbed more slowly into the bloodstream than glucose or sucrose, these are less likely to cause sugar highs and lows, but can cause undesirable side effects like diarrhea)

Calculating the Sugars Inside

Many products today have nutritional labeling. But you must know how to translate the information into measures that you are familiar with. If sugar is listed separately, it is found under "carbohydrate information" and is usually listed in grams. To convert grams of sugar to common measures, just remember:

$$4 \text{ grams of sugar} = 1 \text{ teaspoon sugar}$$

Therefore:

$$12 \text{ grams of sugar} = 1 \text{ tablespoon sugar}$$

$$200 \text{ grams of sugar} = 1 \text{ cup sugar}$$

Selecting Sugar-Smart Foods

Once you get used to looking on the labels, buying sugar smart is as easy as "1, 2, 3."

1. **Read the product name carefully.** Often the name of the product gives a hint of its sugar content. For instance, "pineapples canned in their own juice" has less sugar than "pineapples canned in heavy syrup."
2. **Look for "no sugar added."** When this claim appears, such as on juice labels, the sweetening comes only from the natural fruit inside. Therefore, it's a sugar-smart choice.
3. **Count the number of sweeteners inside.** Learn to spot all of those hidden sugars, regardless of their names. Their number and their placement in the ingredient statement give you a good idea of how much sugar you are buying. Remember, the closer to the front of the statement that an ingredient is listed, the larger the amount of that ingredient in the product.

Inside the supermarket, learn how to spot those sugar-smart foods. Teach the kids which ones to choose, too. Here are a few things to look for:

Canned Fruits: Buy the fruits that are canned in their own juices, not in heavy syrup.

Fruit Juices: Whether you're choosing refrigerated juices or canned ones, select only those with the words "no sugar added."

Frozen Fruit Concentrates: Here again, buy only the concentrates that do not contain added sugars.

At the Fresh Fruit Market: Buy as many fresh fruits as you wish, and let the kids get used to snacking on them instead of a cookie or a slice of cake.

Spreadable Fruits: Instead of the usual jams, jelly, or preserves, try one of the new spreadable fruits. These spreads are made of "all fruit"; they come either unsweetened or sweetened with concentrated fruit juices. Also look for the low-sugar fruit spreads. They often have only 50 percent of the sugar found in regular jam.

Inside the Dairy Case: When buying yogurt, the smart sugar choice is plain, low-fat yogurt. Some nonfat yogurts contain artificial sweeteners and thus have not been used in the recipes in this book. If the kids want a little more flavor, try vanilla yogurt. Naturally, many of the fruit-flavored yogurts are still healthy snacks, but they do rate higher in sugar and calories than the unflavored varieties.

At the Cookie Counter: The healthiest way to satisfy your kid's yen for a cookie is to bake them at home. Try some of the recipes inside this book, like the Black Cherry Stars (see page 38) or the Coconut Moons (see page 31).

However, if you don't have time to bake cookies, there are smart cookie buys in the supermarket. Look for the fruit-filled bars: Choose ones that have sugars listed toward the middle or end of the ingredient listing, and try to find ones that only have, in each serving, 3 grams of fat or less for each 100 calories. Pass by those obvious sugar- and fat-laden cookies such as the sandwich cookies filled with frosting, cookies that are iced, or even those "plain" cookies with sugar sprinkled on top.

At the Bakery: There are some smart ways to choose sugar-smart bakery treats that still have kid appeal. Look for muffins that are high in fruits and fibers, low in sugar. Select the fresh-fruit–filled tarts instead of the whipped cream pies. Choose fruit-filled scones over sugary doughnuts.

Of course, once again, the sugar-smart way to serve cookies, cakes, or breads is to bake them yourself from the recipes inside this book. Nutty Apple Bread is a healthy way to begin the day (see page 117). Ginger Hearts are low on sweetening, high in spice (see page 36). And the Peanut Butter–No Jelly Brownies are chock-full of things much better for you than the regular chocolate fudge variety of brownies (see page 56).

Inside the Ice Cream Freezer: A trip to the ice cream freezer case with the kids can be filled with teachable moments. Point out the better choices: frozen juice pops instead of sugary-sweet popsicles, sorbet instead of rich, creamy ice cream, frozen yogurt pops instead of ice cream on a stick. At home, let the kids help make some of the frozen treats in this book like the Positively Pineapple popsicles (see page 96) and their own home-made Grape Frozen Yogurt Pops (see page 93).

At the Candy Counter: Naturally, it's best to avoid the candy counter. Except for candies sweetened with sorbitol, sugar is almost always a main ingredient in candy. (Fruit roll-ups are an exception.) Consider making candies at home. Try the Chocolate Chip Brittle (see page 141) and the Sugarless Peanut Butter Candy, which is made of dried fruits, coconut, and wheat germ (see page 142).

Reading the Labels for Fat Content

On the Front Panel: First, look on the front panel of the label, right near the product name, for fat clues. But do not be misled by what you see. Presently, the claim "low-fat" has legal meaning only on dairy products or meat. Dairy products such as milk, cheese, and yogurt must contain between 0.4 and 2 percent fat by weight in order to be labeled "low-fat."

However, the current proposals by the Food and Drug Administration and the U.S. Department of Agriculture suggest that fat claims be defined for all products:

- **Fat-free:** less than 0.5 gram of fat per serving and no added fat or oil
- **___ % fat-free:** may be used only in describing foods that qualify as low-fat foods
- **Low-fat:** 3 grams or less fat per serving and per 100 grams of the food
- **Reduced fat:** contains at least 50 percent less fat than the standard, original product

As for cholesterol claims, here are the current guidelines, as issued by the Food and Drug Administration:

- **Cholesterol-free:** 2 milligrams of cholesterol or less per serving
- **Low cholesterol:** 20 milligrams or less of cholesterol per serving
- **Reduced cholesterol:** at least 75 percent less cholesterol than the original form of the product (Note: Cholesterol contents of both products must be given on the label.)

Remember, "no cholesterol" or "low cholesterol" does not necessarily mean "low fat." For instance, many cookies, cakes, and breads on the market today claim "no cholesterol," but that does not necessarily mean that they contain no fat—so keep reading!

In the Nutritional Statement: Naturally, the next fact to read is the nutritional statement, if the product has one. To date, nutritional statements have only been required on products to which nutrients have been added, products that make nutritional claims, and foods for special dietary uses like infant feeding. However, the laws are changing, and more and more foods now carry nutritional statements.

In order to understand the information offered, you need to know that:

$$1 \text{ gram of fat} = 9 \text{ fat calories}$$

With this fact in mind, you can better relate the facts to what you need to know to make a wise choice.

For example, with your kids helping, compare the nutrition information panel on a package of Soft Chocolate Chunk Cookies with the information on a box of Ginger Snaps. You will find the following:

PEPPERIDGE FARM®
SOFT CHOCOLATE CHUNK COOKIES:

Serving Size	1 cookie	Fat	6 grams
Servings per Container	10	polyunsaturated	0 grams
Calories	130	saturated	2 grams
Protein	2 grams	Cholesterol	10 milligrams
Carbohydrate	17 grams	Sodium	45 milligrams

This information tells you that one serving (one cookie) contains 6 grams of fat. Since 1 gram of fat contains 9 fat calories, simply multiply the 6 grams of fat by 9 to find out that each cookie has 54 fat calories. To determine the percent of fat in one serving, simply divide these 54 fat calories by the total amount of calories in each cookie, which is 130, to get 0.42, then multiply by 100 to get 42 percent. This calculation tells you that *42 percent of the calories in these Soft Chocolate Chunk Cookies comes from fat*—definitely not a low-fat treat!

Now, compare this information with the facts on the Ginger Snap label:

NABISCO®GINGER SNAPS:

Suggested Serving Size ½ ounce (approx. 2 cookies)

Servings per Package	32	Fat	1 gram
Calories	60	polyunsaturated	*
Protein	0 grams	saturated	*
Carbohydrate	11 grams	Cholesterol	0 milligrams
		Sodium	80 milligrams

*Contains less than 1 gram.

By applying the same formula, you can quickly see that one serving (two Ginger Snaps) has 1 gram of fat.

Multiplied by 9 fat calories in 1 gram of fat, this equals 9 fat calories. Then divide by 60, which is the total number of calories in each serving, to get 0.15, then multiply by 100 to obtain the percent of calories from fat. *Only 15 percent of the calories in these Ginger Snaps comes from fat.*

Now compare the information:

Soft Chocolate Chunk Cookies = 42 percent of calo-
                                ries come from
                                fat

Ginger Snaps   = 15 percent of calo-
                                ries come from
                                fat

This comparison tells you that the Ginger Snaps are a better low-fat choice than the Soft Chocolate Chunk Cookies.

In the Ingredient Statement: Fats have many names, as we have already discussed in the section, "About Dietary Fats and Cholesterol" (see page 14). As a general rule, low-fat foods should not have any fat listed as the first or second ingredient in the list—and that includes hidden fats such as cocoa butter, eggs, and nuts.

Selecting Fat-Smart Foods

Ready-to-eat desserts and breads, plus many ingredients normally used in making desserts, contain fats. Many of those have been identified in the list of dietary fats (see page 14). You will find that the recipes in this book are lower in fats than standard desserts.

Before buying a prepared, ready-to-eat dessert, look in the ingredient statement to find out how many fats it contains. Here are a few tips for you and your kids to look for:

Inside the Dairy Case: For those puddings, pies, and cakes, reach for the skim milk, 1 percent low-fat milk, or the 2 percent milk. Pass up the whole milk, half-and-half, light cream, and heavy cream. Don't forget buttermilk: It's a great ingredient in many home-baked desserts. Contrary to its name, buttermilk is very low in fat, since it is made from cultured skim milk.

When reaching for cream cheese for dessert making, try the reduced-fat cream cheese instead of the regular kind. It has only half the fat!

Also, look for recipes calling for whipped cream cheese. Ounce per ounce, it goes farther because of the air whipped into it. There are 3 tablespoons in 1 ounce of whipped cream cheese, only 2 tablespoons in regular cream cheese.

Does the recipe call for sour cream? If so, consider half-and-half sour cream products; they often have one-third less fat than regular sour cream. Or, look for one of the new light sour creams being introduced into the marketplace. They are made from sour cream and skim milk and usually have half the fat, or less, and one-third fewer calories than regular sour cream. Better yet, if the recipe is not a baking recipe, experiment with using unflavored, nonfat yogurt instead.

Naturally, when buying yogurt, select one made with low-fat milk or skim milk. An 8-ounce container of low-fat yogurt with fruit contains only 2 grams of fat; whole-milk yogurt with fruit contains 7 grams.

At the Cookie Counter: When comparing fats, the fruit-filled cookies are not only lower in sugar than other cookies but also lower in fats.

> Fig Newtons (a fruit-filled cookie) = 18 percent of
> calories from fat

> Oreos (a chocolate sandwich cookie filled with frosting) = 39 percent of calories from fat

At the Bakery: Buy cakes and pies from the bakery only occasionally. Usually, they are high in fat; in fact, they often even feel buttery or oily to the touch. This generally means they are full of fat—with the exception of angel food cake. Instead, come home and bake up a healthier Strawberry Jam Cake (see page 76). Let the kids help!

Inside the Ice Cream Freezer: Reach for items such as sorbet, ice milk, frozen yogurt, and frozen pudding. They are lower in fat than ice cream. Leave the gourmet ice creams at the store—they are the fattiest ones of all!

At the Candy Counter: Pass up those chocolate treats. Instead, reach for fat-free treats such as hard candies, gumdrops, jelly beans, licorice.

For Snacks: Naturally, you will find tempting snacks throughout the store. Avoid fat-laden snacks like potato chips, nuts, and tortilla chips. Choose rice cakes and pretzels instead. Better yet, come home and pop up some air-popped corn or make some Sunshine Chips (see page 146).

Satisfying That Sweet Tooth—The Healthy Way!

Take a moment to review the 100 recipes in this book. They are perfect for satisfying your child's sweet tooth, and yours too—the low-fat, low-sugar way. Upon reviewing the recipes, you will see that healthy ingredients, tips, and techniques have been used. Here are a few to keep in mind when using other recipe books.

1. When baking, substitute half of the white all-purpose, enriched flour or cake flour with whole wheat pastry or cake flour. For instance, instead of 2 cups of white cake flour, try 1 cup of whole wheat cake flour and 1 cup of white enriched cake flour.
2. Get into the great habit of using fruit juices as sweeteners. These recipes use a variety of juices: apple, orange-pineapple, orange-banana, pineapple, and orange.
3. Apple butter adds a great flavor boost to desserts.
4. Choose the spreadable fruits instead of the sweeter jams and preserves.
5. To grease pans, use a nonstick vegetable cooking spray instead of butter, margarine, or shortening.
6. Use margarine for baking, never butter!
7. Whenever possible, choose recipes without sugar or honey. Many of the recipes in this book fall into this category.
8. Try wheat germ as a healthy garnish for a dessert.
9. When recipes call for cereals, use toasted oat cereals, Corn Chex, or Rice Chex. Avoid recipes using sugar-coated cereals.
10. Use cocoa powder, not chocolate drink mix. Such mixes contain sugar; cocoa powder does not.

·· 2 ··

Cookie Capers

Coconut Moons

Makes 36 cookies
Preparation time: *15 minutes + 1 hour in refrigerator*
Baking time: *12 minutes*

> Cut these coconut snack cookies with a moon-shaped cookie cutter and serve them with fresh fruit at your next barbecue. Kids will love the delicious taste of coconut in these cookies.

1½ **cups unbleached white flour**
1   **cup whole wheat cake flour**
1   **teaspoon baking powder**
1   **teaspoon baking soda**
2   **tablespoons ground cinnamon**
1¼ **cups Domino Brownulated light brown sugar**
½   **cup margarine**
2   **large egg whites**
1   **cup shredded coconut**

1.   Sift together flours, baking powder, and baking soda; set aside.
2.   In a large bowl, combine cinnamon, brown sugar, margarine, and egg whites; mix well using an electric mixer. Gradually add dry ingredients, mixing until a firm dough forms; chill 1 hour.
3.   Preheat oven to 375° F; spray cookie sheet with nonstick cooking spray; set aside.
4.   Roll out dough onto floured board until ¼-inch thick and cut out with moon-shaped cookie cutter. Place cookies on prepared cookie sheets and sprinkle with shredded coconut. Bake 10 to 12 minutes or until golden.
5.   Cool on wire rack. Store in airtight container.

Cashew Cookie Clusters

Makes 48 cookies
Preparation time: 15 minutes
Baking time: 12 minutes

These cookies are light and moist with the nutty taste of cashews, so you can't be sneaky when you eat one of these crunchers.

1	cup unbleached white flour
¾	cup whole wheat cake flour
1	teaspoon baking soda
¼	teaspoon salt
8	ounces margarine
1	cup Domino Brownulated light brown sugar, firmly packed
⅓	cup reduced-calorie sour cream
1	large egg
½	teaspoon vanilla extract
1½	cups cashews, chopped

1.   Preheat oven to 375° F; spray 2 cookie sheets with nonstick cooking spray; set aside.
2.   In a large bowl, sift together flours, baking soda, and salt.
3.   In a medium bowl cream together margarine, brown sugar, sour cream, egg, and vanilla until fluffy; gradually add dry ingredients and mix until well combined; fold in cashews.
4.   Drop by rounded teaspoonfuls and bake 10 to 12 minutes or until lightly golden; cool on wire rack.
5.   Store in airtight container.

Carrot Tops

Makes 40 to 50 cookies
Preparation time: 15 minutes
Baking time: 12 minutes

Carrots can be a terrific way to help make a cookie healthful and moist. These vitamin-enriched snacks are a real crowd pleaser.

2   cups unbleached white flour
2   teaspoons baking powder
¼   teaspoon salt
½   cup margarine
1   tablespoon granulated sugar
1   whole egg, slightly beaten
1   cup carrots, cooked and mashed
2   tablespoons water
1½   teaspoons vanilla extract

1.   Preheat oven to 375° F; spray 2 cookie sheets with nonstick cooking spray; set aside.
2.   In a large bowl, combine flour, baking powder, and salt; set aside.
3.   In a medium bowl, mix margarine, sugar, and egg until fluffy; add carrots, water, and vanilla and mix well.
4.   Drop by rounded teaspoonfuls onto prepared pan and bake 10 to 12 minutes or until light brown.
5.   Cool on wire rack for 10 minutes.
6.   Store in airtight container.

Almond Cookies

Makes 24 cookies
Preparation time: *10 minutes + 1 hour in refrigerator*
Baking time: *20 minutes*

> These easy-to-make almond cookies will become a family favorite. The crunch of almonds in a cookie will perk up any lunch box.

1½	cups unbleached white flour
½	cup margarine
2	tablespoons + 1 teaspoon granulated sugar
1	teaspoon vanilla extract
⅛	teaspoon salt
12	whole almonds, blanched and cut in half

1. On wax paper, sift cake flour; set aside.
2. In a large bowl, cream margarine and sugar until light and fluffy; add vanilla and salt; add flour and mix well. Refrigerate 1 hour or until well chilled.
3. Preheat oven to 375° F; spray a cookie sheet with nonstick cooking spray; set aside.
4. Form into 24 2-inch balls. Place on prepared sheet and press an almond half on each. Bake for 20 minutes.
5. Cool on wire rack for 10 minutes.
6. Store in airtight container.

Sweet and Tart Cookies

Makes 30 cookies
Preparation time: 10 minutes
Baking time: 12 minutes

Kids will eat up this light and tasty cookie. Made with whole wheat flour and oat bran, these goodies are rich in fiber and other nutrients.

¼   **cup margarine**
¼   **cup safflower oil**
½   **cup orange juice**
2   **large egg whites, slightly beaten**
⅓   **cup Domino Brownulated light brown sugar,**
           firmly packed
½   **teaspoon vanilla extract**
1¼   **cups oat bran**
1   **cup whole wheat flour**
1   **teaspoon baking soda**
1   **teaspoon salt**

1.   Preheat oven to 400° F; spray 2 cookie sheets with nonstick cooking spray; set aside.
2.   In a large bowl, combine margarine, safflower oil, orange juice, egg whites, brown sugar, and vanilla; mix very well for 4 to 6 minutes by hand. Add oat bran, flour, baking soda, and salt; mix thoroughly.
3.   Drop by rounded tablespoonfuls onto prepared baking sheet and bake 10 to 12 minutes or until lightly golden.
4.   Cool on wire rack for 10 minutes; store in airtight container.

Ginger Hearts

Makes 4 to 5 dozen
Preparation time: 15 minutes + 1 hour in refrigerator
Baking time: 20 minutes

Make holidays special with these cookies made with crystallized ginger. They have a new, sprightly taste that will wake up your kids' taste buds.

1	cup whole wheat cake flour
1	cup unbleached white flour
1	teaspoon orange extract
¾	teaspoon ground ginger
¼	teaspoon salt
⅛	teaspoon baking soda
¼	cup honey
1½	tablespoons warm water
1	large egg, slightly beaten
¾	cup crystallized ginger, chopped

1.   Sift together flours, orange extract, ginger, salt, and baking soda; set aside.
2.   In a large bowl, combine honey, water, and egg until well mixed; add dry ingredients and mix 2 to 4 minutes with a large spoon until smooth; add crystallized ginger. Wrap dough in plastic wrap and refrigerate for 1 hour.
3.   Preheat oven to 325° F; lightly spray a 13×9×2-inch baking pan with nonstick cooking spray; set aside.
4.   Roll out dough to ½-inch thickness and cut with heart-shaped cookie cutter. Place cookies on prepared baking

pan 2 inches apart; bake 15 to 20 minutes or until lightly golden.

5. Cool on wire rack for 15 minutes.
6. Store in airtight container.

*Black Cherry Stars

Makes 24 cookies
Preparation time: 15 minutes + 1 hour 20 minutes in
*   refrigerator*
Baking time: 15 minutes

A star-shaped cookie cutter makes these sugarless, tangy black cherry cookies perfect for special occasions.

---

1   **8-ounce tub reduced fat cream cheese, room temperature**
¾   **cup reduced calorie margarine, room temperature**
1   **large egg yolk**
1½   **cups whole wheat cake flour**
1   **teaspoon baking powder**
½   **cup black cherry spreadable fruit**

1.   Combine cream cheese, margarine, and egg yolk in a large bowl and mix with an electric mixer until smooth; gradually add flour and baking powder until a stiff dough is formed; wrap dough in plastic wrap and refrigerate for 1 hour.
2.   Preheat oven to 350° F; spray 2 cookie sheets with nonstick cooking spray; set aside.
3.   Divide the dough in half; roll one half between two sheets of wax paper until ½ inch thick; keep remaining dough in the refrigerator.*

*Recipes marked with an asterisk contain no sugar, molasses, or honey.

4.   With a star-shaped cookie cutter, cut out dough and place cookies 1 inch apart on the cookie sheet; using your thumb, make a small indentation in the center of each star; spread a small amount of black cherry spreadable fruit in center.

5.   Refrigerate 20 minutes.

6.   Bake for 15 minutes or until golden brown.

7.   Store in airtight container.

Chocolate Peanut Butter Rounds

Makes 48 cookies
Preparation time: 15 minutes
Baking time: 12 minutes

> If your kids like chocolate and peanut butter together,
> they will reach for handfuls of these cookies. It's a
> delicious way to brighten rainy days.

¾   cup peanut butter
⅓   cup margarine
¼   cup granulated sugar
½   cup Domino Brownulated light brown sugar
1   large egg
¾   teaspoon vanilla extract
1   cup unbleached white flour
½   cup whole wheat cake flour
½   teaspoon baking powder
½   teaspoon baking soda
½   cup low-fat milk
¾   cup semisweet chocolate chips

1. Preheat oven to 375° F; spray cookie sheet with
nonstick cooking spray; set aside.
2. In a large bowl, cream together peanut butter, margarine, granulated sugar, brown sugar, egg, and vanilla. Set
aside.
3. In a medium bowl, sift together flours, baking powder,
and baking soda. Gradually add to peanut butter mixture;
add milk and mix well. Fold in chocolate chips.

4. Drop by rounded tablespoonfuls onto prepared pan. Bake 10 to 12 minutes or until lightly golden.
5. Cool on wire rack.
6. Store in airtight container.

*Apple Butter Cookies

Makes 32 cookies
Preparation time: 15 minutes + 1 hour in refrigerator
Baking time: 10 minutes

> This recipe offers a sugarless new taste in a cookie.
> Look for apple butter in the supermarket and see the
> difference it makes!

¾   **cup nonfat powdered milk**
1   **cup whole wheat cake flour**
1   **teaspoon nutmeg**
¼   **cup raisins**
8   **ounces unsweetened apple butter**
½   **cup peanut butter**
1   **teaspoon vanilla extract**

1.   Preheat oven to 350° F; spray a cookie sheet with
nonstick cooking spray; set aside.
2.   In a large bowl, sift together powdered milk, flour, and
nutmeg; add raisins; set aside.
3.   In a medium bowl, cream together apple butter, peanut
butter, and vanilla; add to dry ingredients and mix well.
4.   Drop by rounded teaspoonfuls onto prepared baking
sheet and bake for 10 minutes.
5.   Cool on wire rack. Refrigerate 1 hour or until chilled.
6.   Store in refrigerator or freezer.

Heavenly Meringue Kisses

Makes 24 servings
Preparation time: 15 minutes
Baking time: 30 minutes

These crunchy, light-as-air kisses will never be too filling.

1   **large egg white**
½   **cup granulated sugar**
⅛   **teaspoon cream of tartar**
1   **cup Corn Chex**

1.   Preheat oven to 350° F; spray 2 cookie sheets with nonstick cooking spray; set aside.
2.   Using an electric mixer, beat the egg white, at medium speed, until frothy.
3.   Gradually add the sugar, 2 tablespoons at a time, beating continuously.
4.   Add cream of tartar and mix until peaks are formed. They should be stiff.
5.   Fold in Corn Chex gently.
6.   Drop mixture, by rounded teaspoonfuls, onto prepared cookie sheets; bake 25 to 30 minutes or until cookies are dry.
7.   Cool 15 minutes; transfer to wire rack.
8.   Store in airtight container.

Orange Juice Cookies

Makes 36 cookies
Preparation time: 15 minutes
Baking time: 10 minutes

Every cookie contains the goodness of orange juice, almonds, and whole wheat. A few of these nutritious cookies make homework fun.

¾   cup granulated sugar
½   cup reduced calorie margarine
1   large egg, slightly beaten
1   large egg white, slightly beaten
½   cup freshly squeezed orange juice
1   tablespoon grated orange peel
2¼ cups whole wheat cake flour
    dash of salt
½   teaspoon baking soda
½   teaspoon finely chopped almonds

1.   Preheat oven to 350° F; spray two cookie sheets with nonstick cooking spray; set aside.
2.   In a large bowl, cream together the sugar and margarine with the back of a large spoon.
3.   Stir into sugar and margarine mixture, the eggs, orange juice, and orange peel; add flour, salt, and baking soda and mix well; fold in almonds.
4.   Drop rounded tablespoons of dough onto baking sheet 2 inches apart; continue with the rest of the dough. Note: Always spray cookie sheets between use.
5.   Bake 10 minutes or until golden brown.
6.   Remove and cool on a rack; store in covered container.

Little Lemon Drops

Makes 24 cookies
Preparation time: 15 minutes
Baking time: 15 minutes

> These light and fluffy cookies, with a hint of lemon,
> will disappear as quickly as you make them.

1   large egg white
1   cup unbleached white flour
1   teaspoon baking powder
¼   cup honey
¼   cup margarine
1   large egg yolk
3   tablespoons fresh lemon juice

1.   Preheat oven to 425° F; spray a 13×9×2-inch baking
pan with nonstick cooking spray; set aside.
2.   In a clean bowl, using a balloon whisk, beat egg white
until stiff peaks form; set aside.
3.   In a small bowl, sift together flour and baking powder;
set aside.
4.   In a large bowl, cream honey and margarine until light;
add egg yolk and lemon juice; mix thoroughly.
5.   Add dry ingredients and beat well; fold in egg white.
6.   Drop by rounded teaspoonfuls onto prepared pan, 2
inches apart, and bake 10 to 15 minutes or until lightly
golden.
7.   Remove and cool on wire rack.
8.   Store in airtight container.

Raisin Squares

Makes 9 squares
Preparation time: 5 minutes
Baking time: 30 minutes

> Pack these light and chewy squares in school lunch boxes. Nothing brings out good taste like the combination of apples and raisins.

2	tablespoons unbleached white flour
1½	teaspoons baking powder
1	large egg
⅓	cup granulated sugar
1	teaspoon vanilla extract
¾	cup raisins, chopped
¼	cup apples, chopped

1.   Preheat oven to 350° F; spray a 9-inch square baking pan with nonstick cooking spray; flour lightly; set aside.
2.   In a small bowl, sift together flour and baking powder.
3.   In a large bowl, combine egg, sugar, and vanilla; mix well; blend in flour mixture.
4.   Stir in raisins and apples.
5.   Pour into prepared pan and bake 25 to 30 minutes or until golden.
6.   Cut into squares and wrap in plastic wrap.
7.   Store in airtight container.

Fruity Cookie Fingers

Makes 36
Preparation time: 10 minutes
Baking time: 30 minutes

> These "fingers" are a chewy, wholesome dessert for the children. Fruit, nuts, and whole wheat give them crunch and fiber.

4	**egg yolks**
¼	**cup honey**
½	**teaspoon vanilla extract**
1	**cup whole wheat cake flour**
¼	**cup raisins**
1	**cup chopped dried fruit**
¼	**cup almonds, chopped**

1. Preheat oven to 300° F; spray a 13×9×2-inch baking pan with nonstick cooking spray; set aside.
2. In a large bowl, mix egg yolks until light and foamy; add honey and vanilla and continue to mix until light and fluffy. Fold in flour, raisins, chopped fruit, and almonds.
3. Pour batter into a pastry bag fitted with a ½-inch opening. Pipe out 3-inch-long strips of dough 3 inches apart on prepared pan. Bake 30 minutes or until lightly golden.
4. Cool on a wire rack 15 minutes.
5. Store in an airtight container.

Granola Nutters

Makes 48
Preparation time: 15 minutes
Baking time: 15 minutes

Peanuts and granola in these cookies combine to make a hearty treat. Keep the cookie jar filled with them year round.

1½   cups unbleached white flour
1   teaspoon baking soda
       pinch of salt
1   cup margarine
1   cup Domino Brownulated light brown sugar, firmly packed
1   large egg
½   teaspoon vanilla extract
2   cups granola
1   cup roasted peanuts, unsalted

1.   Preheat oven to 375° F; spray 2 cookie sheets with nonstick cooking spray; set aside.
2.   In a large bowl, sift together flour, baking soda, and salt.
3.   In a medium bowl, cream margarine, brown sugar, egg, and vanilla until light and fluffy; add dry ingredients and mix well. Stir in granola and peanuts.
4.   Drop by rounded tablespoonfuls onto prepared pan, 2 inches apart, and bake 12 to 15 minutes or until edges are lightly browned.
5.   Cool on wire rack.
6.   Store in airtight container.

Walnut Spicers

Makes 30 cookies
Preparation time: 15 minutes + 1 hour in refrigerator
Baking time: 15 minutes

Kids love the nutty taste of walnuts and spice. Serve these low-sugar cookies with frozen yogurt after the baseball game.

½	cup margarine
2	tablespoons granulated sugar
1	large egg, slightly beaten
1	teaspoon vanilla extract
¾	cup whole wheat cake flour
¾	cup unbleached white flour
1	teaspoon baking powder
¼	teaspoon salt
3	tablespoons ground cinnamon
¾	cup finely chopped walnuts

1: In a large bowl, combine margarine, sugar, egg, and vanilla; mix well; set aside.
2. In a medium bowl, sift together flours, baking powder, and salt. Add to margarine mixture and mix thoroughly. Refrigerate for 1 hour.
3. Preheat oven to 375° F; spray 2 cookie sheets with nonstick cooking spray; set aside.
4. On wax paper, combine walnuts and cinnamon.
5. Roll dough into 2-inch balls. Coat completely by rolling each cookie in walnut-cinnamon mixture.
6. Place on prepared sheets and bake 15 minutes.
7. Cool on wire rack.
8. Store in airtight container.

Double Chip Cookies

Makes 36 cookies
Preparation time: 20 minutes
Baking time: 12 minutes

These cookies are a chewy, double-chip treat made with the whole-grain goodness of oats.

½   **cup margarine**
½   **cup Domino Brownulated light brown sugar, firmly packed**
3   **teaspoons vanilla extract**
1   **large egg white**
1   **cup unbleached white flour**
1½   **cups quick-cooking rolled oats, ground until very fine**
1   **teaspoon baking powder**
1   **teaspoon baking soda**
4   **ounces carob chips**
4   **ounces semisweet chocolate chips**

1. Preheat oven to 375° F; spray 2 cookie sheets with nonstick cooking spray; set aside.
2. In the bowl of an electric mixer, combine margarine, brown sugar, vanilla, and egg white. Beat 2 to 4 minutes until smooth.
3. In a medium bowl, combine flour, rolled oats, baking powder, and baking soda. Mix well.
4. Mixing by hand, gradually add the dry ingredients to the margarine mixture. Fold in chips and stir. Do not overmix.
5. Place dough on wax paper and form 2-inch balls. Place

cookies on prepared sheet and flatten each with the back of a spoon. Bake 10 to 12 minutes or until light brown.

6. Remove to wire rack with spatula and cool for 30 minutes.

7. Store in airtight container.

*Banana Ramas

Makes 36 cookies
Preparation time: *10 minutes*
Baking time: *10 minutes*

Kids who love bananas will want batches of these special cookies for a light and tasty afternoon treat.

1½	cups unbleached white flour
1½	teaspoons baking powder
¼	teaspoon salt
¼	cup margarine
2	small bananas
1	large egg, slightly beaten
3	teaspoons almond extract

1.   Preheat oven to 350° F; lightly spray cookie sheet with nonstick cooking spray; set aside.
2.   In a large bowl, sift together flour, baking powder, and salt.
3.   In a medium bowl, combine margarine, bananas, egg, and almond extract; mix well. Add to dry ingredients and continue to mix for 2 minutes.
4.   Drop by rounded teaspoonfuls onto prepared sheet and bake for 8 to 10 minutes or until lightly golden.
5.   Cool on wire rack 10 minutes.
6.   Store in covered container.

*Apple Drops

Makes 40 cookies
Preparation time: 10 minutes
Baking time: 12 minutes

An apple inside a cookie? These cookies make a great
late-day sugarless treat.

1½   cups unbleached white flour
1½   teaspoons baking powder
½   teaspoon salt
1   large apple, cored, peeled, and mashed
1½   teaspoons vanilla extract
2   tablespoons cinnamon

1.   Preheat oven to 375° F; spray 2 cookie sheets with
nonstick cooking spray; set aside.
2.   In a large bowl, combine flour, baking powder, and salt;
add apple, vanilla, and cinnamon. Mix well.
3.   Drop by rounded teaspoonfuls onto prepared cookie
sheet, 2 inches apart, and bake 10 to 12 minutes or until
lightly golden.
4.   Cool on wire rack for 15 minutes.
5.   Store in airtight container.

*Lemon Oatmeal Cookies

Makes 48 cookies
Preparation time: *10 minutes*
Baking time: *20 minutes*

Cookies can be healthy and taste good, too. Here are sugar-free lemon cookies with the great surprise of raisins.

4   ounces margarine, room temperature
1   large egg, slightly beaten
6   ounces lemon juice
1   cup unbleached white flour
    pinch of salt
1½ teaspoons baking powder
1   cup rolled oats
1   cup golden raisins

1. Preheat oven to 300° F; spray cookie sheets with nonstick cooking spray; set aside.
2. In a large bowl, cream together margarine and egg until light and fluffy; beat in lemon juice.
3. On wax paper, combine flour, salt, baking powder, oats, and raisins; mix well; stir dry ingredients into margarine mixture.
4. Drop rounded tablespoonfuls, 2 inches apart, and bake 15 to 20 minutes.
5. Cool on wire rack.
6. Store in airtight container.

Caramel Cookies 'n' Nuts

Makes 48 cookies
Preparation time: 20 minutes
Baking time: 15 minutes

These are great, wholesome, chewy cookies filled with the goodness of whole wheat, oats, and walnuts.

¾ cup whole wheat cake flour
¾ cup rolled oats
½ teaspoon salt
½ cup margarine
¼ cup granulated sugar
⅓ cup corn syrup
3 tablespoons margarine
½ teaspoon vanilla extract
1½ cups walnuts, chopped

1. Preheat oven to 350° F; spray a 13×9×2-inch baking pan with nonstick cooking spray; set aside.
2. In a large bowl, mix together flour and rolled oats; add salt and set aside.
3. In a medium bowl, cream margarine and sugar; add to flour and oats and blend well. Place dough in prepared pan and bake 15 minutes. Remove from oven and set aside.
4. In a small saucepan, over hot water, combine corn syrup, margarine, and vanilla; stir until smooth. Add walnuts and cool 5 minutes.
5. Spread mixture evenly over baked dough and cut into squares.
6. Cool before serving. Store in airtight container.

Peanut Butter–No Jelly Brownies

Makes 12 servings
Preparation time: 15 minutes
Baking time: 30 minutes

A chewy bite of peanuts are in every square. This
hearty brownie contains no white flour or chocolate;
just watch as your kids eat them up!

½   cup whole wheat cake flour
       dash of salt
½   teaspoon baking powder
¼   teaspoon baking soda
½   cup unsalted margarine, melted
½   cup Domino Brownulated light brown sugar,
       firmly packed
1   whole egg
1   egg white
½   teaspoon vanilla extract
¾   cup chunky peanut butter, room temperature

1.   Preheat oven to 375° F; spray 8×8×2-inch baking pan
with nonstick cooking spray. Set aside.
2.   On wax paper, combine flour, salt, baking powder, and
baking soda; set aside.
3.   In the large bowl of a mixer, cream the margarine,
brown sugar, whole egg, egg white, vanilla, and peanut
butter; continue to mix at low speed until eggs are completely mixed in.

4. Gradually add dry ingredients until well mixed; pour batter into prepared pan.

5. Bake for 30 minutes or until center springs back when touched with the back of a fork; cool for 15 minutes.

6. Cut into squares and serve.

··3··

Snackin' Cakes
and Pies

No-Bake Pink Lemonade Pie

Makes 8 to 12 servings
Preparation time: 5 minutes
Freezing time: 2 to 3 hours

> The chilly goodness of yogurt turns into a frozen treat
> that delights the lemonade connoisseur. Make it a
> great ending to a barbecue.

1   **ready-to-use graham cracker crust**
1   **quart frozen vanilla yogurt, room temperature**
6   **ounces frozen pink lemonade concentrate, thawed**

1. In a blender, combine yogurt and pink lemonade
concentrate until smooth.
2. Pour mixture into pie crust and freeze 2 to 3 hours.
3. Let stand 5 to 10 minutes before serving.

*Nutty Orange Cake

Serves 8
Preparation time: 15 minutes
Baking time: 25 minutes

This healthy, sugarless cake combines the goodness of oats with the nutty flavors of nutmeg and almonds.

2	cups orange juice
1½	cups rolled oats
½	cup margarine
2	eggs
½	teaspoon vanilla extract
2	cups whole wheat cake flour
¾	teaspoon baking soda
1½	teaspoons baking powder
2	teaspoons nutmeg
½	cup ground almonds

1. Preheat oven to 375° F; spray a 13×9×2-inch baking pan with nonstick cooking spray; dust lightly with flour; set aside.
2. In a large bowl, combine orange juice, rolled oats, margarine, eggs, and vanilla until well combined.
3. Add flour, baking soda, baking powder, and nutmeg; mix well; fold in almonds.
4. Pour into prepared pan and bake for 25 minutes or until toothpick inserted in center comes out clean.
5. Cool on rack.

*Recipes marked with an asterisk contain no sugar, molasses, or honey.

Ginger Cupcakes

Makes 12
Preparation time: *20 minutes*
Baking time: *30 minutes*

> This spicy cupcake is simple to make and it's rich in fiber and whole-grain goodness.

½   cup margarine
½   cup Domino Brownulated light brown sugar,
       firmly packed
1   large egg, slightly beaten
½   cup honey
1½   cups whole wheat cake flour
¾   cup unbleached white flour
1   teaspoon baking soda
1   teaspoon baking powder
2   teaspoons ground ginger
1   teaspoon salt
¾   cup milk

1. Preheat oven to 350° F; line cupcake pans with paper liners; set aside.
2. In a large bowl, cream together margarine, brown sugar, egg, and honey until light and fluffy; set aside.
3. Sift together flours, baking soda, baking powder, ginger, and salt; add to margarine mixture, alternating with small amounts of milk; mix until smooth.
4. Pour into prepared tins and bake for 30 minutes or until lightly brown.
5. Cool on wire rack for 10 minutes. Can be frozen.

Applesauce in a Square

Makes 12 servings
Preparation time: 15 minutes
Baking time: 50 minutes

Kids will love to get their hands on this moist, nutritious dessert treat that has the delicious taste of apples.

¾   cup all-purpose flour, sifted
1   cup whole wheat cake flour
2   teaspoons baking soda
¾   teaspoon nutmeg
¾   teaspoon cinnamon
¼   teaspoon ground cloves
¾   cup Domino Brownulated light brown sugar,
     firmly packed
1   large egg
1   large egg white
½   cup reduced calorie tub margarine
12 ounces chunky applesauce, room temperature

1.   Preheat oven to 350° F; spray 9×9×2-inch square baking pan with nonstick cooking spray; dust lightly with flour; set aside.
2.   On wax paper, combine flours, baking soda, nutmeg, cinnamon, cloves, and brown sugar; mix well with a fork; set aside.
3.   In a large bowl of an electric mixer, combine egg, egg white, margarine, and 6 ounces of the applesauce; mix well.
4.   Gradually add the dry ingredients, beating at low speed, scraping the sides of the bowl with a rubber spatula; continue to beat for 2 to 4 minutes.

5.   Add the remaining 6 ounces of applesauce and beat for 1 minute.

6.   Pour evenly into prepared pan.

7.   Bake 50 minutes; cake is done when toothpick inserted in center comes out clean.

8.   Cool 15 minutes in pan; remove to wire rack to cool completely.

9.   Cut into 12 squares and serve.

Chocolate Honey Cake

Serves 12 to 14
Preparation time: 20 minutes
Baking time: 60 minutes

An old-fashioned honey cake is always welcomed.
This wholesome version is thick and hearty.

¾   **cup unbleached white flour**
1   **cup whole wheat cake flour**
1   **teaspoon baking soda**
1   **teaspoon salt**
½   **cup margarine**
3   **ounces unsweetened chocolate, melted**
⅔   **cup honey**
1   **teaspoon vanilla extract**
1   **large egg**
1   **large egg white**
½   **cup warm water**

1.   Preheat oven to 350° F; spray a 9×5×3-inch loaf pan
with nonstick cooking spray; dust with flour; set aside.
2.   Sift together flours, baking soda, and salt; set aside.
3.   In a large bowl, cream margarine, chocolate, honey,
vanilla, egg, and egg white until well combined.
4.   Gradually add flour mixture and mix until batter is
smooth; add water if necessary.
5.   Bake in prepared pan for 60 minutes or until toothpick
inserted in center comes out clean.
6.   Cool on wire rack for 15 minutes before serving.

Chunks of Cherries

Makes 36 squares
Preparation time: 15 minutes
Baking time: 30 minutes

This tangy cherry dessert goes perfectly with a glass
of cold milk. Each square contains a minimal amount
of sugar.

1½   cups fresh or frozen cherries, washed and pitted
½   cup granulated sugar
½   teaspoon baking soda
1   teaspoon baking powder
1½   cups whole wheat cake flour
¼   teaspoon salt
¾   cup low-fat milk
3   egg whites, whipped until firm

1.   Preheat oven to 375° F; spray 13×9-inch baking pan
with nonstick cooking spray; set aside.
2.   To prepare cherry mixture: combine cherries with ¼
cup of sugar in a food processor; pulse until the mixture is
thick; set aside.
3.   In a large bowl, combine ¼ cup sugar, baking soda,
baking powder, flour, and salt; mix well.
4.   Stir in milk and egg whites until well combined.
5.   Fold in cherry mixture; spread evenly in prepared pan.
6.   Bake 30 minutes or until lightly golden.
7.   Invert pan on wax paper to remove; while cooling, cut
into squares with a sharp knife.

*Apple Cheesecake

Serves 8
Preparation time: *20 minutes*
Baking time: *90 minutes*

> An elegant kids' dessert, this lightweight cheesecake
> is the perfect finish to that special meal.

Crust
¼   cup low-fat milk
1   large egg yolk
1   cup whole wheat cake flour
¾   teaspoon baking powder
1½   teaspoons cinnamon

Filling
2   cups chopped apple
3   large eggs
2   cups fat-free cottage cheese
2   tablespoons unbleached white flour
1   teaspoon lemon juice
2   teaspoons vanilla extract

1.   Preheat oven to 350° F; spray a springform baking pan
with nonstick cooking spray; set aside.
2.   To make crust: In a medium bowl, combine milk, egg
yolk, flour, baking powder, and cinnamon with a large fork;
press evenly into bottom of the springform pan.
3.   Place chopped apple in blender and blend until smooth.
4.   To make filling: Pour eggs, blended apple, cottage
cheese, flour, lemon juice, and vanilla into the bowl of an
electric mixer and beat until smooth.

5. Pour apple mixture into springform pan and bake 90 minutes or until lightly golden.

6. Cool 15 minutes before removing.

7. Refrigerate until serving.

Blueberry Honey Cake

Serves 8
Preparation time: 15 minutes
Baking time: 60 minutes

This moist snacking cake that's chock-full of blueberries is a treat when served warm.

½   **cup margarine**
½   **cup honey**
2   **large egg yolks**
½   **teaspoon vanilla extract**
2   **large egg whites**
⅛   **teaspoon cream of tartar**
1   **cup unbleached white flour**
1   **cup whole wheat flour**
1   **teaspoon baking powder**
1   **cup low-fat milk**
2   **cups blueberries, lightly dusted with flour**

1.   Preheat oven to 350° F; spray 8-inch square baking pan with nonstick cooking spray; dust lightly with flour; set aside.
2.   In a large bowl, cream margarine until fluffy; gradually add honey, egg yolks, and vanilla; mix well; set aside.
3.   In a medium bowl, with a balloon whisk, beat egg whites and cream of tartar until whites are stiff, not dry.
4.   On wax paper, sift together flours and baking powder; set aside.
5.   Add dry ingredients to margarine-honey mixture, alternating with small amounts of milk. Add ½ the egg whites and mix well.
6.   Fold in blueberries plus remaining ½ egg whites.

7. Pour into prepared pan and bake for 60 minutes or until toothpick inserted in center comes out clean.

8. Cool on wire rack.

9. Cut into squares and serve.

Coconut Cupcakes

Makes 12
Preparation time: 15 minutes
Baking time: 25 minutes

Kids love cupcakes. This moist, honey-sweetened treat is made with fiber-rich whole wheat flour and shredded coconut.

½	cup honey
¼	cup low-fat sour cream
¼	cup margarine, softened
1¾	cups whole wheat cake flour
1½	teaspoons baking powder
1	teaspoon baking soda
¾	cup milk
3	large egg whites
1	teaspoon vanilla extract
3½	cups shredded coconut

1. Preheat oven to 350° F; line a 12-cupcake pan with paper liners; set aside.
2. In medium bowl, beat together honey, sour cream, and margarine; set aside.
3. In a large bowl of an electric mixer, combine flour, baking powder, and baking soda; add honey–sour cream mixture, alternating with small amounts of milk, and mix for 1 minute; add egg whites and vanilla; mix another 2 minutes; fold in coconut.
4. Pour into cupcake tin and bake 25 minutes or until toothpick inserted in center comes out clean.
5. Remove from pan and cool on wire rack for 10 minutes.

Pineapple Cheese Pie

Serves 8 to 10
Preparation time: 10 minutes + 2 to 3 hours in refrigerator
Baking time: 25 minutes

> This cool pineapple treat contains only one table-
> spoon of honey. Best of all, this creamy cheesecake is
> easy to make and delicious for the whole family.

Crust
¼	cup margarine
¼	cup wheat germ
2	cups shredded coconut

Filling
16	ounces pineapple chunks, packed in their own juice, drained
8	ounces plain yogurt
8	ounces light cream cheese
1	tablespoon honey

1.   To make crust: Preheat oven to 300° F. In a medium
bowl combine margarine, wheat germ, and coconut; mix
well. Press crust evenly into the bottom of a 9-inch pie plate.
Bake 20 to 25 minutes or until lightly golden. Cool for 15
minutes.

2.   For filling: In a blender, combine pineapple chunks,
yogurt, cream cheese, and honey; blend at medium speed
until smooth.

3.   Pour filling into prepared pie crust. Chill in the refrigerator 2 to 3 hours before serving.

Applesauce Raisin Cake

Makes 18 servings
Preparation time: 20 minutes
Baking time: 45 minutes

> Cut this moist, healthful cake into squares for a
> terrific afternoon snack. Applesauce makes this cake
> chewy and brings out the best flavors.

¾	cup light tub margarine
¾	cup Domino Brownulated light brown sugar, firmly packed
1	large egg, slightly beaten
2	cups whole wheat cake flour
¼	cup unbleached white flour
½	teaspoon salt
1½	teaspoons baking powder
1½	teaspoons allspice
1	cup raisins, steamed over boiling water for 10 minutes
1½	cups unsweetened applesauce

1.   Preheat oven to 325° F; spray a 13×9-inch baking pan
with nonstick cooking spray; set aside.
2.   In a large bowl, cream margarine and brown sugar until
light and fluffy; add egg and mix well.
3.   In a medium bowl, sift together flours, salt, baking
powder, and allspice; mix well. Fold in raisins.
4.   Add flour-raisin mixture to margarine and mix well.
Add applesauce and blend well.

5. Pour batter into prepared pan and bake 45 minutes or until toothpick inserted in center comes out clean.

6. Cool 15 minutes in pan.

7. Remove and cool completely on wire rack before serving.

*Strawberry Jam Cake

Serves 12
Preparation time: 15 minutes
Baking time: 35 minutes

> Kids will delight in this hearty jam-filled cake with a
> glass of cold milk. It's a strawberry lovers' dessert.

½   **cup unbleached white flour**
2   **cups whole wheat cake flour**
1   **teaspoon baking soda**
1   **teaspoon allspice**
2   **teaspoons cinnamon**
½   **cup margarine**
3   **large eggs**
1½   **cup fruit-sweetened strawberry jam**
¼   **cup buttermilk**

1.   Preheat oven to 350° F; spray an 8-inch square baking
pan with nonstick cooking spray; dust lightly with flour; set
aside.
2.   In a medium bowl, combine flours, baking soda,
allspice, and cinnamon.
3.   In a large bowl, cream margarine until light and fluffy;
add eggs, one at a time, and mix well. Add flour mixture to
margarine mixture, then add jam and buttermilk and mix
well.
4.   Pour into prepared pan and bake for 35 minutes or until
toothpick inserted in center comes out clean.
5.   Cool in pan and then place on wire rack for 30 minutes.
6.   Cut into squares and serve.

·· 4 ··

Wonderful Wiggles

*Sweet Bread Pudding

Makes 6 servings
Preparation time: 25 minutes
Baking time: 40 minutes

A sugar-free bread pudding that's full of flavor. Add some vanilla frozen yogurt on special occasions.

1½   cups low-fat milk
2   cups plain bread cubes, stale
1½   cups frozen apple juice concentrate, thawed
1   egg, beaten
1   egg white, beaten
¼   teaspoon ginger
¼   teaspoon nutmeg
¾   cup seedless raisins

1.   Preheat oven to 375° F; spray 6 individual custard cups with nonstick cooking spray; set aside.
2.   In a small saucepan, over low heat, heat the milk until boiling; remove to a large bowl.
3.   In a large bowl with the milk, soak the bread cubes; let stand 15 minutes; add apple juice concentrate, egg, egg white, ginger, nutmeg, and raisins; mix well.
4.   Divide mixture equally into 6 custard cups; place cups in a 13×9-inch baking pan with 2 inches of water; bake for 40 minutes or until knife inserted into custard comes out clean; cool for 10 minutes, then place in the refrigerator to cool completely.
5.   Unmold before serving.

*Recipes marked with an asterisk contain no sugar, molasses, or honey.

*Perfectly Pears

Serves 6
Preparation time: 10 minutes

> Enjoy the great taste of pears in a creamy pudding.
> Top with berries for a special treat.

4   cups fresh pears, peeled and chopped
¼   cup cornstarch
¾   teaspoon nutmeg

1.   Place chopped pears in a blender and whip for 1 to 2 minutes until smooth; add cornstarch and nutmeg and beat for 2 more minutes.

2.   Pour pear mixture in top of double boiler, stirring constantly, until mixture reaches boiling and thickens; remove from heat.

3.   Pour into 6 individual dishes and serve warm.

Peach Whip

Makes 10 servings
Preparation time: 15 minutes
Refrigeration time: 8 hours

2 cups fresh, ripe peaches, peeled and sliced
3 tablespoons honey
½ teaspoon almond extract
1 3-ounce package peach flavored Jell-O
1 cup boiling water
¾ cup frozen vanilla yogurt

1. In a blender, combine peaches, honey, and almond extract; blend until smooth; set aside.
2. In a large bowl, dissolve Jell-O in boiling water and stir until completely dissolved; stir in peach mixture and chill for two hours, uncovered.
3. Pour mixture into blender and beat 5 minutes at highest speed until almost doubled in volume; fold in frozen vanilla yogurt.
4. Pour into 10 paper cups and chill 6 hours or overnight.

*Orange Custard

Makes 6 servings
Preparation time: *10 minutes*
Baking time: *50 minutes*

Orange juice is not just for the morning. Treat your youngster to this smooth orange custard.

1	cup frozen orange juice concentrate, thawed
3	eggs
1	egg yolk
½	cup half-and-half
1	cup whole milk
1	tablespoon grated orange peel
6	orange sections, for garnish

1. Preheat oven to 325° F.
2. In a large bowl, combine orange juice concentrate, eggs, egg yolk, half-and-half, and whole milk; mix well; add grated orange rind.
3. Pour into individual custard cups and place in baking pan with ½ inch water; bake 45 to 50 minutes or until knife inserted around edges comes out clean; remove.
4. Cool in refrigerator.
5. Serve with an orange section on top of each.

Chocolate Oatmeal Pudding

Makes 8 servings
Preparation time: 20 minutes
Baking time: 40 minutes

This healthy and tasty dessert pudding will give your kids the benefits of oat bran with the added surprise of chocolate.

6	slices oatmeal bread, cut into cubes
¾	cup Domino Brownulated light brown sugar, firmly packed
½	cup cocoa powder (not drink mix)
½	cup oat bran
½	teaspoon nutmeg
3	cups low-fat milk
1	tablespoon margarine
1	teaspoon vanilla extract

1.   Preheat oven to 350° F; spray a 3-quart casserole dish with nonstick cooking spray; set aside.
2.   Place the bread cubes on the bottom of the casserole dish; set aside.
3.   In a medium saucepan, combine brown sugar, cocoa powder, oat bran, nutmeg, and 1 cup of milk; mix well. Cook over medium heat, stirring constantly, for 2 minutes; add 2 cups milk, margarine, and vanilla; remove from heat.
4.   Pour liquid over bread cubes and bake for 40 minutes; cool on wire rack; serve warm.

Raspberry Clouds

Makes 6 servings
Preparation time: 15 minutes + 1 hour in refrigerator

A light, dreamy berry dessert. Watch as the raspberries melt in your child's mouth.

2   large egg whites
1   envelope unflavored gelatin
¼   cup cold water
½   cup boiling water
2½   cups raspberries, washed
2   teaspoons lemon juice
¾   teaspoon granulated sugar

1.   In a clean bowl, beat egg whites with a large balloon whisk until stiff; set aside.
2.   In a medium bowl, sprinkle gelatin over cold water; allow to soften for 8 minutes; add boiling water and stir until completely dissolved.
3.   In a food processor, combine raspberries, lemon juice, and sugar; puree. Stir in gelatin mixture. Cool 10 to 15 minutes and beat again until frothy.
4.   Fold in stiff egg whites and pour into dessert dishes. Chill until set, about 1 hour.

Grape Cream Dessert

Makes 6 servings
Preparation time: 15 minutes + 1 hour in refrigerator

> Any kid who likes grape juice will love this dessert.
> There is a sweet and tart creamy taste in every
> spoonful.

1	envelope unflavored gelatin
1½	cups unsweetened grape juice
4	teaspoons granulated sugar
1½	cups vanilla yogurt

1.   In a large saucepan, combine gelatin and grape juice
until gelatin is softened; cook over low heat until completely dissolved. Remove.
2.   Stir in sugar. Cool until it starts to set; fold in yogurt
and spoon into individual dessert glasses. Refrigerate until
completely set, about 1 hour.

*Strawberry Smash

Serves 8 to 10
Preparation time: 30 minutes + 3 hours in refrigerator

> The supreme strawberry dessert. Kids will love the
> taste and creamy texture of this sugar-free treat.

1   **tablespoon unflavored gelatin**
½   **cup boiling water**
2   **tablespoons fresh lemon juice**
16   **ounces fresh, ripe strawberries, rinsed and stems**
        removed
1   **cup plain yogurt**

1.   In a large bowl, stir the gelatin into the water and lemon
juice; stir constantly until dissolved.
2.   With the back of a large spoon, gently mash the
strawberries into the warm gelatin; mix thoroughly. Cool for
30 minutes.
3.   Mix again for 2 minutes; fold in yogurt and pour into a
1-quart mold. Chill for 3 hours.

*Little Apple Soufflé

Serves 6
Preparation time: 15 minutes
Baking time: 20 minutes

A sophisticated kids' dessert, it's irresistibly the best tasting apple in town.

2	cups unsweetened applesauce
3	tablespoons frozen orange juice concentrate, thawed
¼	teaspoon cinnamon
1	cup golden raisins
4	egg whites
½	teaspoon nutmeg

1. Preheat oven to 350° F.
2. In a large bowl, combine applesauce, orange juice concentrate, and cinnamon; mix well.
3. In individual 6-ounce custard cups, spoon 1 tablespoon of the applesauce mixture and divide raisins evenly on top.
4. In a clean bowl, with a large balloon whisk, beat the egg whites until stiff peaks form; fold whites into remaining applesauce mixture; pour evenly into 6 custard cups; sprinkle tops with nutmeg.
5. In a baking pan filled with 2 inches of water, place custard cups and bake for 20 minutes until tops are lightly golden.
6. Remove and serve warm.

*Cinnamon-Vanilla Pudding

Serves 8
Preparation time: 20 minutes + 2 to 3 hours in refrigerator

When you don't want to serve a sugar-filled dessert, this cinnamon-sweetened pudding is perfect. Make this healthful treat ahead of time and have it ready when school's out.

---

2 cups milk
2 tablespoons cornstarch
1 large egg, slightly beaten
2 teaspoons vanilla extract
2 teaspoons margarine, melted
2 teaspoons ground cinnamon

1. In a medium saucepan, over low heat, combine milk and cornstarch until thickened. Remove from heat.
2. In a small bowl stir the egg with 2 tablespoons of the milk mixture and stir. Return to saucepan and cook until thick; cool 8 to 12 minutes.
3. Blend in vanilla, melted margarine, and cinnamon; stir well.
4. Pour into individual dessert dishes and chill for 2 to 3 hours.
5. Serve chilled and garnish with a sprinkle of cinnamon.

·· 5 ··

Chillers

*Red, White, and Blueberry Dessert

Makes 4 servings
Preparation time: 10 minutes

> Fresh berries and yogurt combine to make this cold
> and colorful dessert look as good as it tastes.

1½   **cups low-fat frozen vanilla yogurt, thawed**
1   **cup whole fresh blueberries, washed**
1   **cup whole fresh raspberries, washed and cut in
        halves**
8   **whole berries, to garnish**

1.   In the bottom of a parfait glass, spoon 2 tablespoons
vanilla yogurt.
2.   Layer ¼ of the blueberries; spoon another 2 tablespoons of the vanilla yogurt.
3.   Layer ¼ of the raspberries; top with a layer of the
yogurt; repeat in each of 4 glasses.
4.   Garnish each with fresh berries and serve.

*Recipes marked with an asterisk contain no sugar, molasses, or honey.

91

Banana Delights

Makes 4 servings
Preparation time: 15 minutes
Freezing time: 1 hour

This light and sweet dessert makes bananas taste heavenly. Kids will enjoy a whole new way to eat one of their favorite fruits.

2	large bananas, sliced into ½-inch slices
1	teaspoon orange juice
¼	teaspoon sugar
1	teaspoon vanilla extract
¼	teaspoon cinnamon
2	large egg whites
⅛	teaspoon cream of tartar
4	paper cups

1. In a blender, combine banana slices, orange juice, sugar, vanilla, and cinnamon; blend at medium speed for 2 minutes until smooth; transfer to a large bowl.
2. In a clean bowl, beat egg whites with a large balloon whisk and add cream of tartar; continue to beat until whites are stiff but not dry.
3. Fold egg whites *gently* into banana mixture; pour evenly into paper cups; place in freezer for one hour to set.

*Grape Frozen Yogurt Pops

Makes 8 servings
Preparation time: 5 minutes
Freezing time: 2 hours

It's a low-fat after-school delight. It's cold, it's purple, and it's the perfect simple treat.

---

2   **cups frozen vanilla yogurt, softened**
6   **ounces frozen grape juice concentrate, thawed**
8   **paper cups**
8   **popsicle sticks**

1. In a large bowl, combine frozen yogurt and grape juice concentrate; mix well until no lumps appear.
2. Pour yogurt mixture evenly into paper cups; place in freezer for one hour; remove.
3. Place a popsicle stick in the center of each cup; place back in the freezer until completely frozen.
4. To eat: Carefully remove the paper cup by gently running a knife around the edge and then invert the cup to remove the pop.
5. Serve immediately.

*Watermelon Building Blocks

Serves 6
Preparation time: 5 minutes
Freezing time: 12 hours

Here's summer fruit in a chilling new way. Kids will love to satisfy their summertime appetites with this full-of-fun dessert.

1   **cup frozen orange juice concentrate, thawed**
1½   **cups watermelon, cut into small pieces, seeds removed if possible**
¼   **cup water**

1.   Place orange juice concentrate, watermelon cubes, and water in a blender; blend 2 minutes on high speed.
2.   Pour into plastic ice cube trays and freeze thoroughly.
3.   Remove from trays and serve blocks frozen in a bowl. Let the kids use their spoons to chip away at dessert.

*Orange Boats

Makes 6 servings
Preparation time: *15 minutes*
Freezing time: *12 hours*

Refreshing fresh fruit and yogurt fill those "I'm hungry" blues. Let the kids help you make this vitamin-packed dessert.

6	large oranges
2	cups frozen vanilla yogurt
¼	cup orange juice concentrate, thawed
¼	cup fresh orange juice (reserved from oranges)
1	teaspoon grated orange peel
6	seedless grapes, halved for garnish

1. To prepare orange boats: Cut a 1-inch circular section from the top of each orange; with a teaspoon, scoop out the pulp, squeeze, and strain juice; set aside.
2. In a large bowl, combine vanilla yogurt, orange juice concentrate, fresh squeezed orange juice, and grated orange peel; mix well.
3. Fill each orange boat ¾ of the way up with the vanilla-orange mixture; freeze overnight.
4. To serve: Let boats stand at room temperature for 10 to 20 minutes; garnish with grape halves.

*Positively Pineapple

Makes 6 servings
Preparation time: 5 minutes
Freezing time: 12 hours

> Pops are forever! Kids will love this fun fruit pop with their friends after school.

4   ounces pineapple, fresh or canned, packed in its own juice, chopped into small pieces
4   popsicle molds

1. Pour chopped pineapple into a blender and blend at high speed for 3 minutes until smooth.
2. Pour into individual popsicle molds and freeze for 12 hours or overnight.

Papaya Ices

Makes 8 servings
Preparation time: 5 minutes
Freezing time: 2 hours

This tropical fruit dessert is rich in vitamin A. It's easy to make and kids love the taste.

---

4   ripe papayas
½   cup granulated sugar
½   cup lemon juice
2   egg whites

1. Scoop out the pulp of the papayas into a large bowl; mix with sugar and lemon juice.
2. In a clean bowl, beat egg whites until stiff but not dry; fold into papaya mixture.
3. Pour into individual popsicle molds and freeze 2 hours or until completely frozen.

*Fruit Cocktail Slushy

Makes 8 servings
Preparation time: 5 minutes
Freezing time: 1 hour

Keep this easy twist on an old favorite in the freezer, ready to serve, when the kids come in after playing baseball.

14   large ice cubes
16   ounces fruit cocktail, packed in its own juice, drained

1.   Place ice cubes in a blender or food processor; put on high speed until crushed.
2.   Gradually spoon in fruit cocktail and blend well.
3.   Spoon mixture into 8 paper cups and freeze 1 hour. Should not be frozen solid.
4.   Serve in cups with a spoon.

*Ring Around a Cantaloupe

Serves 4 to 6
Preparation time: 10 minutes
Freezing time: 2 hours

> This healthy frozen fruit sundae will cool your kids
> off on a hot afternoon.

1	**ripe cantaloupe**
1	**cup vanilla yogurt**
6	**ounces dried fruit bits**
	shredded coconut, to garnish

1. Slice cantaloupes crosswise to make ½-inch rings.
Remove rind.
2. Place cantaloupe rings on a baking sheet and freeze 1 to
2 hours.
3. In a small bowl, combine yogurt with dried fruit bits
and mix well.
4. Place 2 to 3 frozen rings on each dessert plate. Fill the
centers with the yogurt-fruit mixture.
5. Garnish with shredded coconut.

Easy Lemon Sherbet

Serves 8
Preparation time: 15 minutes
Freezing time: 1 hour

This terrific make-ahead dessert is a tart sherbet that kids will love when they come home from school.

1¼   **cups frozen lemonade concentrate, thawed**
2   **large egg yolks**
2   **cups plain yogurt**
2   **large egg whites, beaten until fluffy**

1.   In a blender, combine lemonade concentrate and egg yolks and blend at low speed for 1 minute. Add yogurt and blend at medium speed for 10 to 20 seconds; pour into container and freeze until slushy. Remove and fold in egg whites.
2.   Place in a covered container and freeze.
3.   Serve in ice cream dishes.
Note: Sherbet should not be frozen solid.

••6••

Fabulous Fun Fruits

Sticky Fruit

Makes 6 servings
Preparation time: 15 minutes

This sticky fun treat is a new way to give your kids vitamin C. It will disappear every time.

3	tablespoons honey
1½	cups white grape juice
4	navel oranges, peeled and cut into segments
4	pink grapefruits, peeled and cut into segments
4	ounces raisins

1.   In a clean bowl, combine honey and white grape juice; stir to combine.
2.   Add the orange and grapefruit segments and toss with a large spoon to coat well; add raisins and chill for 45 minutes.
3.   Spoon into dessert bowls and serve cold.

*Granola Fun Fruit

Makes 4 servings
Preparation time: 12 minutes

> Here's a dessert that pleases both parents and kids.
> What a great combination of cool, crisp fruit and
> crunchy granola!

16	watermelon balls
16	honeydew balls
16	cantaloupe balls

Granola Mix

1	cup rolled oats
1	cup flaked coconut
1	cup sunflower seeds, without shells
1	tablespoon vegetable oil

1.   Using a melon baller, prepare melon balls. Chill the
fruit balls in a large, covered container.
2.   In a medium bowl, toss together rolled oats, coconut,
sunflower seeds, and vegetable oil; mix well.
3.   In 4 dessert dishes, place 4 of each kind of melon ball
on bottom of dish; sprinkle generously with granola mix;
serve.

*Recipes marked with an asterisk contain no sugar, molasses, or honey.

*Fruit Kebobs

Makes 6 servings
Preparation time: 10 minutes

When you make fruit fun to eat, it will disappear as quickly as any sweet confection. These kebobs are coated with wheat germ for added crunch and fiber.

2   large navel oranges, peeled and separated into sections
1   16-ounce can of pineapple chunks packed in its own juice, drained; reserve the juice
2   large bananas, cut into ¼-inch rounds
1   mango, peeled and cut into pieces
½   large cantaloupe, in balls
½   large honeydew melon, in balls
6   green grapes
6   red grapes
½   cup wheat germ

1. On skewer, arrange the fruit starting with the oranges.
2. Place finished kebobs on a large plate and pour pineapple juice to coat completely.
3. On a separate plate, spread the wheat germ; roll each kebob in the wheat germ until coated and serve.

*Colorful Cantaloupes

Makes 8 servings
Preparation time: 10 minutes

A burst of color brightens the center of a chilled cantaloupe. Rich in vitamins A and C, this refreshing dessert will please adults or kids anytime.

2   large, ripe cantaloupes
1½   cups raspberries, washed and cut in half
1½   cups green grapes, halved
½   cup red grapes
¼   cup frozen orange juice concentrate, thawed

1.   Cut the cantaloupes in quarters, remove the seeds, and set aside.
2.   In a large bowl, combine raspberries, green grapes, and red grapes; pour orange juice concentrate over fruit mixture; toss with a large spoon and chill.
3.   Spoon equal amounts of fruit into the center of each cantaloupe; serve immediately.

Peachy Cobbler

Makes 8 servings
Preparation time: *15 minutes*
Baking time: *50 minutes*

Old-fashioned peach cobbler has been enjoyed by
kids for centuries. This one has almost no added
sugar.

6	large peaches, peeled, cored, and sliced into ¼-inch slices
3	tablespoons lemon juice
¾	cup unbleached white flour
⅛	cup wheat germ
	pinch of salt
3	tablespoons margarine, cut into pieces
2	tablespoons granulated sugar
⅓	teaspoon baking soda
½	cup plain yogurt

1. Preheat oven to 375° F; spray 8-inch baking pan with
nonstick cooking spray; set aside.
2. Place peach sections in prepared pan and sprinkle with
lemon juice.
3. In a large bowl, combine flour, wheat germ, salt,
margarine, sugar, and baking soda; mix well. Stir in yogurt.
4. Pour mixture over peach sections and bake for 50
minutes or until top is lightly brown.
5. Cool on rack.

Smiling Apples

Makes 4 servings
Preparation time: 10 minutes

An apple a day is still a great idea. Make this easy
dessert and always get a big smile.

**2   large, red-skinned apples, cored and sliced into
        quarters**
¼   cup peanut butter
16   tiny marshmallows

1.   On a large sheet of wax paper place the apple quarters;
spread ½ teaspoon of peanut butter on one side of each
quarter.
2.   Place 4 tiny marshmallows on top of the peanut butter
on four of the apple quarters.
3.   Place remaining four quarters, peanut butter side down,
on top of each apple with marshmallows to make a
"sandwich."
4.   Press together and serve immediately.

*Pineapple Blues

Serves 4
Preparation time: 3 minutes

Fruit and yogurt is a tried and true combination that
never fails to please. This combo is especially pretty
and delicious.

8   ounces fresh blueberries, rinsed
8   ounces unsweetened, crushed pineapple packed in
        its own juice, drained; reserve juice
4   ounces plain yogurt

1.   In a large bowl, toss together blueberries and pineapple;
set aside.
2.   In a small bowl, combine plain yogurt and reserved
pineapple juice; mix well.
3.   Spoon fruit mixture into 4 dessert glasses and top each
with ''sweetened'' yogurt.

*Island Peaches

Makes 4 servings
Preparation time: 5 minutes

This yummy island dessert is easy to fix, and the peaches go crunch!

4   large, ripe peaches, peeled
½   cup shredded coconut
¼   cup wheat germ

1.   Slice peaches into thin slices.
2.   In a large bowl, toss shredded coconut and wheat germ; mix well. Add peach sections and toss to coat.
3.   Serve chilled.

Banana Warm-Ups

Serves 4
Preparation time: 5 minutes

Serving this treat is a quick and easy way to make any banana lover smile. It's a yummy, warm snack that treats fruit a whole new way.

---

2   teaspoons margarine
2   teaspoons vegetable oil
1   tablespoon maple syrup
4   ripe bananas, cut into 2-inch rounds

1.   In a medium skillet, heat the margarine, oil, and maple syrup, stirring constantly.
2.   Add the bananas, cooking 2 minutes on each side.
3.   Serve warm.

Lip-Smacking Baked Pears

Serves 6
Preparation time: 15 minutes
Baking time: 30 minutes

A new twist on an old favorite. Kids will welcome these warm and spicy treats on a cold afternoon.

---

3   **cups white grape juice**
¼   **cup granulated sugar**
2   **tablespoons grated lemon peel**
2   **tablespoons ground nutmeg**
1   **tablespoon ground cinnamon**
6   **large, ripe pears, peeled, halved, and cored**

1.   Preheat oven to 350° F.
2.   In a heavy saucepan, combine grape juice, sugar, lemon peel, nutmeg, and cinnamon; cover and warm over low heat until sugar is completely melted; uncover and transfer to an oven-proof casserole dish.
3.   Place pears, round side up, in mixture and bake for 30 minutes, basting frequently until tender.
4.   Cool 10 minutes; serve warm.

*Baking Apple Bites

Makes 4 servings
Preparation time: 10 minutes
Baking time: 30 minutes

A warm treat to cure rainy day blues. Nuts and raisins make this dessert burst with flavor.

3   **tablespoons chopped walnuts**
3   **tablespoons raisins**
1   **teaspoon sunflower seeds**
2   **teaspoons ground cinnamon**
4   **apples, cored**

1.   Preheat oven to 350° F; spray an oven-proof casserole dish with nonstick cooking spray; set aside.
2.   In a small bowl, combine walnuts, raisins, sunflower seeds, and cinnamon; mix well.
3.   Place the cored apples in the baking dish. Fill their centers with the nut-raisin mixture; sprinkle any remaining on top.
4.   Cover with aluminum foil and bake 30 minutes or until tender.
5.   Cool 5 to 10 minutes before serving.

Special Spicy Plums

Makes 2 servings
Preparation time: 10 minutes

Plums make a fine dessert or snack. The spicy
sweetness will entice your kids.

½   **cup water**
1   **stick cinnamon**
1   **whole clove**
¾   **teaspoon granulated sugar**
3   **firm, purple plums, peeled and quartered**

1.   In a medium saucepan, combine water, cinnamon stick,
clove, and sugar; bring to a boil and add plums; reduce heat
and cook 4 to 6 minutes.
2.   Remove plums with a slotted spoon; remove any
remaining pits; serve warm.

··7··

Lovin' Muffins and Best Breads

Nutty Apple Bread

Makes 1 loaf
Preparation time: *20 minutes*
Baking time: *65 minutes*

> Try this healthful bread that's delicious and hearty. Kids just adore a thick slice of apples and nuts.

¼	cup peanut butter
2	tablespoons margarine
2	large eggs
⅓	cup honey
1¼	cups whole wheat flour
1¼	teaspoons baking soda
2	teaspoons allspice
¾	cup quick-cooking rolled oats
¼	cup wheat germ
⅔	cup plain yogurt
1	cup apples, chopped fine
¼	cup chopped walnuts

1. Preheat oven to 350° F; spray a 9×5-inch loaf pan with nonstick cooking spray; set aside.
2. In a large bowl, mix peanut butter, margarine, eggs, and honey until smooth; set aside.
3. In a medium bowl, sift together flour, baking soda, and allspice; add rolled oats and wheat germ; mix thoroughly.
4. Combine flour mixture with peanut butter mixture; add yogurt, apples, and walnuts. Blend well.
5. Pour batter into prepared pan. Bake 60 to 65 minutes or until toothpick inserted in center comes out clean.
6. Remove loaf from pan and cool.
7. Store in plastic wrap.

Zucchini Munchin' Muffins

Makes 12
Preparation time: 15 minutes
Baking time: 20 minutes

Serve this guilt-free snack any time of the day. Kids
will love to bite into this marvelous, moist muffin.

1	cup whole milk
2	tablespoons honey
2	tablespoons corn oil
1	large egg
1½	cups unbleached white flour
½	cup oat bran
⅛	cup granulated sugar
1	teaspoon baking powder
½	teaspoon baking soda
½	teaspoon allspice
½	teaspoon nutmeg
1¼	cups grated zucchini, drained

1. Preheat oven to 400° F; spray muffin tins with nonstick
cooking spray; set aside.
2. In a medium bowl, mix the milk, honey, corn oil, and
egg; set aside.
3. In a large bowl, mix together flour, oat bran, sugar,
baking powder, baking soda, allspice, and nutmeg; add milk
mixture and mix well. Stir in grated zucchini.
4. Pour into prepared pans and bake for 15 to 20 minutes
or until lightly golden.
5. Serve warm.

*Super Sesame Muffins

Makes 12
Preparation time: 15 minutes
Baking time: 15 minutes

> Serve these crunchy muffins. Calcium-rich sesame seeds make the delicious difference.

2	large eggs
1	large egg white
¼	cup margarine, softened
¾	cup orange juice
1	cup whole wheat cake flour
1	cup unbleached white flour
1	teaspoon baking soda
¾	cup sesame seeds

1. Preheat oven to 350° F; spray muffin tins with nonstick cooking spray; set aside.
2. In a large bowl, combine eggs, egg white, margarine, orange juice, flours, and baking soda; mix well. Stir in sesame seeds.
3. Spoon mixture into prepared tins and bake 10 to 15 minutes or until tops are golden; remove.
4. Cool on wire rack for 10 minutes. Can be frozen.

*Recipes marked with an asterisk contain no sugar, molasses, or honey.

Plump Pumpkin Bread

Makes 1 loaf
Preparation time: 15 minutes
Baking time: 60 minutes

This thick and hearty bread satisfies hungry snackers.
Serve a thick, warm slice and keep the cold weather
outside.

1½   **cups fresh or canned pumpkin**
½   **cup vegetable oil**
½   **cup honey**
1¾   **cups whole wheat flour**
       pinch of salt
1   **teaspoon baking soda**
¾   **teaspoon cinnamon**

1.   Preheat oven to 350° F; spray 8×4-inch loaf pan with
nonstick cooking spray; set aside.
2.   In a large bowl, combine pumpkin, oil, and honey; mix
well; stir in flour, salt, baking soda, and cinnamon; mix
well.
3.   Pour into prepared pan and bake for 60 minutes or until
toothpick inserted in center comes out clean.
4.   Cool on wire rack; slice and serve.

Yummy Mini Muffins

Makes 24 muffins
Preparation time: 20 minutes
Baking time: 20 minutes

> These molasses-sweetened snacks are rich in fiber
> and filled with the goodness of oats and whole wheat.

⅓   cup molasses
½   cup oil
2   whole eggs
1   tablespoon grated lemon rind
2   tablespoons fresh lemon juice
⅔   teaspoon cream of tartar
1   cup whole wheat cake flour
1   teaspoon nutmeg
1½   cups rolled oats

1.   Preheat oven to 350° F; spray mini muffin tins with
nonstick cooking spray; set aside.
2.   Combine molasses, oil, and eggs in a large bowl; mix
until smooth; set aside.
3.   Add lemon rind and lemon juice.
4.   On wax paper, combine cream of tartar, flour, nutmeg,
and rolled oats; add dry ingredients to oil mixture and mix
well.
5.   Spoon into prepared muffin tins only ⅔ of the way up;
bake for 20 minutes or until toothpick inserted in center
comes out clean.
6.   Cool on rack; store in a warm, dry place.

*Orange Pineapple Muffins

Makes 12 muffins
Preparation time: 15 minutes
Baking time: 25 minutes

Surprise your kids with a muffin that's got the sun inside. This vitamin-packed snack will please the fruit lovers in your home.

2	large eggs
1	large egg white
½	cup orange juice
1	cup margarine, softened
1	cup unbleached white flour
1½	cups whole wheat flour
1	teaspoon baking soda
1	teaspoon baking powder
1	8-ounce can pineapple chunks packed in its own juice, drained and chopped

1. Preheat oven to 300° F; spray muffin tin with nonstick cooking spray; dust lightly with flour; set aside.
2. In a large bowl, beat eggs, egg white, orange juice, and margarine until smooth; add flours, baking soda, and baking powder and mix well.
3. Fold in pineapple chunks.
4. Spoon mixture into muffin tins and bake for 20 to 25 minutes or until lightly brown.
5. Cool on wire rack.

Corn Bread Squares

Makes 12 squares
Preparation time: 15 minutes
Baking time: 30 minutes

Corn bread is a family favorite all over the country. Serve these after a hearty meal and watch them disappear.

1	**cup unbleached white flour**
¾	**cup cornmeal**
2	**tablespoons baking powder**
½	**teaspoon salt**
1	**cup low-fat milk**
1	**large egg, slightly beaten**
¼	**cup honey**
2	**tablespoons margarine, melted**

1.   Preheat oven to 400° F; spray an 8×8-inch square baking pan with nonstick cooking spray; set aside.
2.   In a large bowl, combine flour, cornmeal, baking powder, and salt; mix well.
3.   Add milk, egg, honey, and margarine and mix well.
4.   Pour into prepared pan and bake 25 to 30 minutes or until lightly golden.
5.   Cool on rack 10 minutes; cut into squares and serve warm.

*Apple Muffins

Makes 12 muffins
Preparation time: *10 minutes*
Baking time: *20 minutes*

These sugar-free, sweet muffins are great to share with friends at lunchtime.

½   cup whole wheat cake flour
½   cup unbleached white flour
2   teaspoons baking powder
¼   teaspoon salt
1   large egg, slightly beaten
1   cup unsweetened apple juice
2   tablespoons vegetable oil
¾   cup chopped apple

1.   Preheat oven to 400° F; spray muffin tin with nonstick cooking spray; set aside.
2.   In a large bowl, combine flours, baking powder, and salt; mix well with a large fork; set aside.
3.   Add egg, apple juice, and vegetable oil and mix for 2 minutes or until well combined. Fold in chopped apple. Pour batter into prepared tin and bake for 20 minutes or until firm to the touch.
4.   Cool on wire rack for 10 minutes.

Radical Raisin Bran Muffins

Makes 12
Preparation time: 15 minutes
Baking time: 35 minutes

> These moist and hearty muffins are welcome morning, noon, and night. Kids will take them hot off the shelf.

1	**cup unbleached white flour**
¾	**cup bran**
4	**teaspoons baking powder**
½	**teaspoon salt**
¾	**cup raisins**
½	**cup whole milk**
3	**tablespoons honey**
2	**teaspoons vegetable oil**
1	**large egg, slightly beaten**

1. Preheat oven to 425° F; spray muffin tin with nonstick cooking spray; set aside.
2. In a large bowl, combine flour, bran, baking powder, salt, and raisins; mix well.
3. Add milk, honey, vegetable oil, and egg; mix lightly to make a moist batter. Pour into muffin tin and bake 25 to 35 minutes or until lightly browned.
4. Cool on wire rack for 15 minutes.

Cocoa Shortbread

Makes 30 squares
Preparation time: 10 minutes
Baking time: 20 minutes

This quick shortbread is a snacker's delight. Serve these moist squares with berries or frozen yogurt.

1	cup margarine, softened
1	cup powdered sugar
1½	teaspoons vegetable oil
1	cup whole wheat cake flour
1	cup unbleached white flour
½	cup unsweetened cocoa (not drink mix)

1.   Preheat oven to 325° F; spray a 9×9×2-inch square cake pan with nonstick cooking spray; set aside.
2.   In a large bowl, cream together margarine, sugar, and vegetable oil; beat until fluffy. Gradually stir in flours and cocoa; mix well.
3.   Place batter into prepared pan and grease evenly; prick with fork and bake for 20 minutes or until firm; cut into squares.
4.   Remove and cool on wire rack.

*The Absolute Applesauce Muffin

Makes 9 jumbo muffins
Preparation time: 15 minutes
Baking time: 25 minutes

This moist and delicious muffin is the perfect snack for the really hungry after-school bunch. The big taste of apple is in every bite.

1	cup applesauce
1	large egg, slightly beaten
¼	cup vegetable oil
1¼	cup whole wheat cake flour
2	teaspoons baking powder
¼	teaspoon salt
1	teaspoon nutmeg

1. Preheat oven to 375° F; spray 9-muffin tin with nonstick cooking spray; set aside.
2. In a large bowl, combine applesauce, egg, and vegetable oil and mix lightly; set aside.
3. In a medium bowl, combine flour, baking powder, salt, and nutmeg; mix well; add to applesauce mixture and mix; batter should be moist and lumpy; spoon into prepared muffin tin and bake for 20 to 25 minutes or until lightly golden.
4. Remove and cool on wire rack.

··8··

Little Bites

Goodness Gracious Granola

Makes 8 servings
Preparation time: 5 minutes
Cooking time: 6 minutes

> Let your kids help microwave a delicious granola. It's the best wholesome snack in town.

1	**cup rolled oats**
½	**cup toasted sesame seeds**
¼	**cup Domino Brownulated light brown sugar, firmly packed**
¼	**cup sliced almonds**
¼	**teaspoon ground nutmeg**
1	**medium banana**
⅓	**cup vegetable oil**
½	**cup raisins**

1.   In a microwave-safe bowl, combine oats, sesame seeds, brown sugar, almonds, and nutmeg; mix well; set aside.

2.   In a small bowl, mash the banana with the vegetable oil until thoroughly mixed. Pour the banana-oil mixture over the dry ingredients; stir with a large spoon until well mixed.

3.   Microwave, on high power, for 2 minutes, then stir well. Continue to microwave, uncovered, for 2 minutes, stirring occasionally. Finish cooking for 2 more minutes.

4.   Remove dish from microwave and fold in raisins. Let granola stand for 1 hour until cool. Store in an airtight container.

*Tropical Crackers

Makes 24 crackers
Preparation time: 10 minutes
Baking time: 12 minutes

> These crispy crackers are made for snacking. Kids
> will love the hint of citrus in each crunchy bite.

1	cup whole wheat pastry flour
2	cups unbleached white flour
1	cup orange-pineapple juice
½	cup vegetable oil

1.   Preheat oven to 375° F; generously spray a 13×9-inch
baking sheet with nonstick cooking spray. Set aside.
2.   In a large bowl, combine whole wheat flour, 1 cup
white flour, orange-pineapple juice, and oil. Mix well with
a large fork. Add remaining 1 cup of white flour until soft,
pliable dough is formed.
3.   Roll out dough to ½-inch thickness; cut with round
cookie cutter. Place on prepared sheets and bake 10 to 12
minutes or until lightly golden.
4.   Cook on wire rack.
5.   Store in airtight container.

*Recipes marked with an asterisk contain no sugar, molasses, or honey.

No-Bake Coconut Bars

Makes 36 bars
Preparation time: 10 minutes

When time is short and your kids have friends coming over, make these terrific treats. They're hearty, delicious crowd pleasers.

2   cups quick-cooking rolled oats
1   cup peanut butter
1   cup shredded coconut
1   cup granulated sugar
½   cup whole milk
¼   cup unsweetened cocoa
½   cup margarine
1   teaspoon vanilla extract

1.   Spray a 13×9-inch baking pan with nonstick cooking spray; set aside.
2.   In a small bowl, combine rolled oats, peanut butter, and coconut; mix well. Set aside.
3.   In a large saucepan, over low heat, cook sugar, milk, cocoa, margarine, and vanilla; stirring constantly, bring to a boil and remove from heat.
4.   Add peanut butter mixture and stir well.
5.   Spread the mixture in prepared pan and score with a knife.
6.   Cover and chill in refrigerator for ½ hour.
7.   Cut into squares to serve.

Walnut Snacking Drops

Makes 36
Preparation time: 15 minutes
Baking time: 45 minutes

A great taste combination in every drop. Walnuts and chocolate will please the most finicky taste buds.

2	**cups unbleached white flour**
½	**teaspoon salt**
1	**cup margarine**
¼	**cup honey**
1	**teaspoon vanilla extract**
1½	**cups walnuts, finely chopped**
½	**cup cocoa powder**

1.   Preheat oven to 350° F; spray 13×9×2-inch cookie sheet with nonstick cooking spray, set aside.
2.   On wax paper, sift together flour and salt; set aside.
3.   In a medium bowl, cream together the margarine, honey, and vanilla extract; mix well until smooth. Add flour mixture and chopped walnuts and mix.
4.   On wax paper, form dough into 1-inch balls; place 2 inches apart on cookie sheet and bake for 45 minutes.
5.   Cool on wire rack for 10 minutes.
6.   Roll drops in cocoa powder and store in airtight container.

Apple Chip Chunks

Makes 16 servings
Preparation time: 10 minutes

This chewy bar is a high-fiber snack with the wonderful flavors of peanut butter and apples. It's delicious when served with vanilla frozen yogurt.

⅓   **cup peanut butter**
1   **6-ounce package of apple bits**
4   **cups toasted oat cereal**

1.   Line a 13×9×2-inch baking pan with wax paper; spray with nonstick cooking spray; set aside.
2.   In a large saucepan, combine peanut butter and apple bits, cooking over low heat, stirring constantly, until smooth; remove from heat; gradually add toasted oat cereal; stir well.
3.   Spoon into prepared pan and press evenly to cover the bottom of the pan completely.
4.   Cool 30 minutes; cut into 16 squares.

Pineapple Sticks

Makes 12 servings
Preparation time: 15 minutes
Baking time: 35 minutes

Fun fruit bars make the best take-along snacks.
They're a great way to incorporate fruit into your
child's day.

1¼	cups whole wheat cake flour
	dash of salt
¼	teaspoon baking soda
¼	teaspoon baking powder
¼	cup sugar
3	ounces reduced calorie margarine, softened
¾	cup egg substitute
½	teaspoon vanilla extract
12	ounces pourable pineapple fruit
⅓	cup finely chopped dried apricots
¼	cup finely chopped walnuts

1.   Preheat oven to 350° F; spray 13×9×2-inch baking pan
with nonstick cooking spray; dust lightly with flour; set
aside.
2.   On wax paper, combine flour, salt, baking soda, and
baking powder.
3.   In the large bowl of an electric mixer, beat sugar and
margarine until light and fluffy; add egg substitute and
vanilla and mix well.
4.   Gradually add dry ingredients and pourable fruit and
beat on medium speed until well blended.

5.   Fold in dried apricots and chopped walnuts.

6.   Pour batter into prepared pan and bake for 35 minutes or until toothpick inserted into center comes out clean.

7.   Cool on rack for 10 minutes; cut into squares.

8.   May be wrapped in plastic wrap and frozen.

Popcorn on a Stick

Makes 8 servings
Preparation time: 25 minutes
Cooking time: 5 minutes

> A fun, high-fiber treat that's just right for snack time.
> Kids will love this sweet popcorn "lollipop."

4   tablespoons margarine
½   cup Domino Brownulated light brown sugar,
        firmly packed
¼   cup corn syrup
5   cups popcorn, popped
1   cup dried fruit mix, chopped
½   cup rolled oats
8   popsicle sticks

1. In a large saucepan, over medium heat, combine
margarine, brown sugar, and corn syrup; cook 2 minutes,
stirring constantly until well combined; remove from heat.
2. With a large spoon, stir in popcorn, dried fruit, and
rolled oats until thoroughly coated.
3. On wax paper, shape into 8 individual balls, insert a
popsicle stick into the center of each. Cool for 15 minutes.
4. Wrap each in plastic wrap and store in a dry place.

Snow Bars

Makes 24 servings
Preparation time: 20 minutes
Baking time: 20 minutes

Pack these chewy snacking bars in lunch boxes. Kids will eat up the fruity sweetness.

---

3   large eggs, slightly beaten
1¼   cups honey
1½   cups unbleached white flour
1   teaspoon baking powder
1   teaspoon vanilla extract
4   cups dried fruit, chopped
1   cup peanuts, chopped
        powdered sugar, to coat

1.   Preheat oven to 350° F; spray 13×9×2-inch baking pan with nonstick cooking spray; set aside.
2.   In a large bowl, with a wooden spoon, combine eggs and honey; mix well. Add flour, baking powder, and vanilla and mix well; fold in dried fruit and peanuts.
3.   Pour batter into prepared pan and flatten to ¼ to ½ inch; bake for 20 minutes; cool.
4.   Cut into 2-inch bars and roll each bar in powdered sugar.
5.   Store in airtight container.

*Fabulous Fruit Chillers

Makes 12 servings
Preparation time: 3 minutes
Freezing time: 12 hours

> Are your kids very hungry and in the mood for something cold and sweet? Frozen fruit snacks can't be beat. Keep bags of chillers frozen and ready to munch.

1   bunch of seedless green grapes, washed and
        separated
2   large semi-ripe bananas, peeled and cut into ½-
        inch slices

1.   Place grapes and banana slices on a 13×9-inch cookie sheet and cover with plastic wrap; freeze overnight.
2.   Transfer to a large plastic zip-lock bag and keep frozen until ready to eat.

Chocolate Chip Brittle

Makes 30 servings
Preparation time: 10 minutes
Baking time: 25 minutes

Here's a snack that will be impossible to eat quietly. When your kids beg for candy, serve this homemade confection instead.

¼   **cup margarine**
½   **tablespoon granulated sugar**
1   **teaspoon salt**
1   **teaspoon vanilla extract**
1   **cup unbleached white flour**
½   **cup walnuts, chopped**
½   **cup semisweet chocolate chips or carob chips**

1.   Preheat oven to 375° F; spray a jelly roll pan with nonstick cooking spray; set aside.
2.   In a medium bowl, combine margarine, sugar, salt, and vanilla; beat until smooth.
3.   Mix in flour, walnuts, and chips and mix until well combined.
4.   Spoon mixture into prepared pan and bake for 25 minutes; cool in pan for 15 minutes; break into pieces.
5.   Store in airtight container.

*Sugarless Peanut Butter Candy

Makes 48 pieces
Preparation time: 5 minutes

What can you do when only something sweet will
satisfy? Let them pop a few of these sugarless
''candy'' drops in their mouths and watch them smile.

1½ cups creamy peanut butter
¾   cup dried apricots, chopped into small pieces
½   cup dried pineapple, chopped into small pieces
½   teaspoon nutmeg
½   cup shredded coconut
¼   cup wheat germ

1. In a large bowl, combine peanut butter, apricots,
pineapple, and nutmeg; mix well.
2. In a small bowl, combine the coconut and wheat germ;
set aside.
3. Form fruit mixture into 2-inch balls and roll each in
coconut–wheat germ. Place on flat pan and cover with
plastic wrap.
4. Refrigerate and serve cold.

*Poppy Seed Crackers

Makes 48 crackers
Preparation time: 15 minutes
Baking time: 20 minutes

Kids will love to spread peanut butter or cottage cheese on these whole-grain crackers. Serve them alone or with fruit.

1   cup whole wheat flour
1   cup quick-cooking oatmeal
⅓   cup vegetable oil
4   tablespoons unsweetened apple juice
1   cup poppy seeds

1.   Preheat oven to 325° F; spray 2 cookie sheets with nonstick cooking spray; set aside.
2.   In a large bowl, combine flour and oatmeal; add oil and apple juice and mix well; add poppy seeds and continue to mix until soft, pliable dough is formed.
3.   Roll out dough to ⅛ inch between two sheets of wax paper and cut into 2-inch squares; prick with fork; place on prepared sheets and bake 15 to 20 minutes or until brown around the edges.
4.   Cool on cookie sheet and store in a covered container.

*Peppy Oven-Baked Potato Chips

Makes 4 dozen
Preparation time: 10 minutes
Baking time: 60 minutes

Show kids how much fun it is to make homemade potato chips. This snacking chip is the ultimate hunger stopper.

---

3   medium baking potatoes
salt substitute
paprika

1. Preheat oven to 325° F.
2. Scrub potatoes well and slice into ⅛-inch slices. (Using a food processor fitted with a slicing blade will save you time.)
3. On a large baking rack covered with aluminum foil, place potato slices in a single layer.
4. Sprinkle lightly with salt substitute and paprika; bake for 60 minutes or until crisp; cool.
5. Store in a large paper bag.

*Sesame Snack-Ums

Makes 36 pieces
Preparation time: 15 minutes

Give your kids a sugarless ''candy'' that's good for them. This chewy treat takes a while to eat.

¾   **cup dried fruit, chopped**
½   **cup sesame seeds**
½   **teaspoon cinnamon**
1¼   **cup peanut butter**
½   **cup wheat germ**

1.   In a large bowl, combine dried fruit, sesame seeds, and cinnamon. Add peanut butter until well combined.
2.   On wax paper, shape into 2-inch balls and roll in wheat germ.
3.   Place on flat baking sheet and chill for one hour before serving.

*Sunshine Chips

Makes 36 chips
Preparation time: 5 minutes
Drying time: 8 hours

Fruit is every parent's ideal snack. Watch how quickly these banana chips replace other snacking chips.

3   **firm bananas, cut into ½-inch slices**
1½   **cups unsweetened orange juice concentrate, thawed**

1.   Preheat oven to 150° F; leave door open 2 inches; line a cookie sheet with wax or parchment paper.
2.   Dip banana slices into orange juice concentrate and place on prepared cookie sheet.
3.   Place in oven with the door open, for 8 hours, until completely dry and chewy.
4.   Store in airtight container.

*Crunchy Fingers

Makes 16
Preparation time: 10 minutes

> Let the kids help you make these "fingers," and learn
> how to snack healthy. Pick them up with a toothpick
> and make them more fun to eat!

2   cups toasted oat flakes
½   cup peanut butter
2   tablespoons vegetable oil
4   slices oatmeal or whole wheat bread, toasted and
        cut into 1-inch strips

1.   Place toasted oat flakes in a sealable plastic bag, crush
with a rolling pin, and pour onto wax paper.
2.   In a medium saucepan, over low heat, combine peanut
butter and vegetable oil until easy to stir; transfer to a
shallow bowl.
3.   Dip each toast strip into the melted peanut butter and
coat completely. Roll each strip in crushed oat flakes until
no peanut butter shows. Cool on a wire rack.

·· 9 ··

Shake 'Em Up

*Peachy Keen Shake

Makes one serving
Preparation time: 3 minutes

Finish off an all-American meal with a fruity shake that's quick to fix and delicious to sip.

½ cup low-fat milk
1 whole peach, pitted and cut into ¼-inch pieces
¼ teaspoon ground ginger

1. Place all ingredients in a blender; blend at high speed for 2 minutes until thick and smooth.
2. Serve in a tall glass.

*Recipes marked with an asterisk contain no sugar, molasses, or honey.

151

Shakin' Strawberries

Makes 6 servings
Preparation time: 10 minutes

> This healthy, thick shake that's full of fresh strawber-
> ries is a favorite among the "shake set."

2	**cups whole strawberries**
1½	**tablespoons sugar**
3	**cups low-fat milk**
1	**cup strawberry frozen yogurt, softened**

1.   In a colander, wash the berries thoroughly under cold water; transfer to a medium bowl and mash the berries with the back of a large spoon; set aside.
2.   Combine the mashed berries and sugar; gradually add the milk and beat with a rotary beater until smooth; spoon in the frozen yogurt and continue to beat for 3 minutes.
3.   Spoon into tall glasses and garnish with a fresh strawberry half.

*Banana Blitz

Makes 2 servings
Preparation time: 3 minutes

This delicious milk shake offers bursts of bananas that will tickle your tongue.

1   banana, frozen and cut into 1-inch slices
1   cup low-fat milk
¼   teaspoon vanilla extract
¼   teaspoon cinnamon
¼   teaspoon nutmeg, for garnish

1.   Place all ingredients except nutmeg into a blender and blend for 1 minute until mixture is thick and creamy.
2.   Pour into 2 tall glasses and sprinkle ⅛ teaspoon nutmeg on each before serving.

*Tropical Shake-Up

Makes 2 servings
Preparation time: 5 minutes

Make summer days special when you whip up this tropical fruit shake. The combination of island fruits is a vitamin-packed treat.

¾   cup plain yogurt
¼   cup fresh mango, cut into ¼-inch pieces
¼   cup fresh papaya, cut into ¼-inch pieces
½   cup fresh pineapple, cut into ¼-inch chunks

1. Place all ingredients in a blender and blend until smooth.
2. Serve in iced glasses.

*Apple Thick Shake

Makes 4 servings
Preparation time: 5 minutes

> Try this creamy, calcium-rich apple shake instead of
> plain apple juice.

1   **6-ounce can unsweetened apple juice concentrate,**
     thawed
1   **cup apple, skin removed and cut into ¼-inch pieces**
2   **cups plain yogurt**
1   **large egg**
½   **teaspoon ground cinnamon, to garnish**

1.   Place all ingredients in a blender; blend until smooth
and creamy.
2.   Serve in chilled glasses and sprinkle with cinnamon.

Chocolate Raspberry Drink

Preparation time: 5 minutes

This drink will give your kids a quick pick-me-up
after a long day at school. Yummy is the only word
for the combination of berries and chocolate.

¾   **cup fresh raspberries, washed and chopped**
⅓   **cup vanilla yogurt**
2   **tablespoons unsweetened cocoa powder**

1.   Put all ingredients in a blender and blend at high speed
for 30 seconds or until frothy.
2.   Serve in chilled glasses or mugs.

*Cherry-Pineapple Smoothie

Makes 2 servings
Preparation time: 5 minutes

> This smoothie is perfect as an after dinner treat. Kids will finish every drop of this "cherry-full" dessert.

½   **cup plain yogurt**
½   **cup cherries, pitted**
⅓   **cup unsweetened pineapple juice**
1   **whole cherry, cut in half, for garnish**

1. Place yogurt, cherries, and pineapple juice in a blender and blend at high speed for 2 minutes until thick and creamy.
2. Serve in frosted glasses and garnish with cherry halves.

About the Authors

ROBIN ZINBERG received her technical training at the New York Restaurant School in New York City. She has worked as a test kitchen associate at *Weight Watchers Magazine* and runs a successful private and corporate catering business in Manhattan. As an elementary school teacher and the mother of two young sons, she has plenty of first-hand knowledge of what kids like—or refuse—to eat and plenty of opportunities to kid-test her recipes.

BETH ALLEN, president of her own food marketing communications firm in New York City, frequently writes, speaks, and consults on food, nutrition, and health issues. She has contributed to such publications as the *New York Times*, *Woman's Day*, and *Self* magazine. Additionally, she has created national food programs for numerous major food corporations such as The Grand Union Company, Kraft General Foods, and the United Brands Company.